NOT JUST FISHING

"A ONE-OF-A-KIND BOOK SURE TO INTEREST EVERY FISHERMAN"

GARRY COOPER

Copyright © 2014 Authored By Garry Cooper
All rights reserved.

ISBN: 099048730X
ISBN 13: 9780990487302

TABLE OF CONTENTS

Striped Bass Fishing	1
Trolling for stripers and catching them two at a time	3
Trolling for stripers in shallow water near shore – my best striper-trolling tip	4
Using a bait runner reel with large, live bait – my favorite way to catch striped bass	6
Using a bobber for catching stripers	9
Fishing stripers with cut bait	10
All You Need to Know about Sturgeon Fishing!	13
How to clean and cook a sturgeon	21
Salmon Fishing The Most Popular and Unusual Techniques for Slaying Them	24
"Long lining" – the most popular way to shore fish for salmon	25
Lure fishing from shore – an unusual but effective method	28
A tricky way to fish a flatfish from shore	31
Back trolling – the most effective way to catch salmon from a boat	33
Trout and Steelhead	37
Catching steelhead from shore in swift water	38
The ever-important trout "drift"	40
Catching wild trout in streams	41

Catching planted trout in streams	45
Best lures for stream fishing and how to fish with them	47
A sure-fire method for fishing from shore in lakes with Power Bait	49
A secret technique for trolling near shore for lake trout	51

Black Bass Fishing (Largemouth, smallmouth, others) — 54

Sight fishing for bass in the spring on their nests	55
A couple of the most-effective methods for using Senko worms	57
Simple advice and tips for using crankbaits	59
Spinnerbaits – don't leave home without them	61
Fishing small farm ponds	63

Catfish, Crappie, Perch, Bluegill, and Pan Fish — 65

Catching perch, bluegill, rock bass, and other pan fish – The "meeting them halfway" technique	65
Catching crappie with minnows and jigs	68
Catching bullhead and yellow catfish	71
Catching channel catfish using lures and bait	73

Shad Fishing with Lightweight Fishing Gear —

A Fishing Trip Worth Making Every Year	74
How to fish for shad in the river	75

Diving and spear fishing — no need for scuba equipment for this fun! — 78

How to spearfish – the spear gun, the Hunt, the gear, and the spear	79
How to dive for abalone – an in-depth "how-to-snorkel" lesson, too	85
How to dive for sea urchins for sushi – get your very own free "uni"	93
Fishing with hooks when diving – bet you never heard of doing this before	95
Octopus story – an exciting diving safety lesson I wanted to share with you	98
Ten best safety tips for diving – this could save your life	101

Other Ocean Fishing and Fun ... 103
    Fishing for rockfish from shore ... 103
    Catching surfperch off of the beach ... 106
    Getting mussels off the rocks at low tide for chowder and fishing bait ... 108
    Clam digging with your homemade clam pump ... 111
    More clam-digging tips ... 115
    Using a poke pole for eels and rockfish – I dated a girl in college with that same face! ... 117
    Rock picking abalone on a low tide ... 120
    Catching rock crab in tide pools ... 124
    Catching rock crab on mud flats at low tide ... 125

Other Fun and Off-the-wall fishing ... 128
    Frog gigging – a dying sport ... 128
    Jugging for snapping turtles and catfish ... 134
    Catching crawfish out of rice fields by hand and with traps in rivers ... 136

Some Other Excellent Fishing Tips for You ... 141
    Using a trailer hook when trolling – great for bass and trout ... 141
    How to bait minnows and baitfish for different purposes ... 142
    Learning how to fish from scratch – some helpful guidance for the beginner ... 143
    Fish spawning temperature chart – a great chart for your shop wall ... 145

Introduction: How to Use This Book and What It's All About

Welcome, my friend! This book is written not only for fishermen of all skill levels but also for any outdoorsman who enjoys short stories about outdoor sporting activities ranging from the usual to the not-so-common. Tips on frog gigging, spear fishing in the ocean, jugging for turtles, and getting mussels, clams, urchins, and abalone, as well as unique and proven ways to catch about any type of fish, is what you can expect from this book. I guarantee that all fishermen, no matter how long they have been fishing or how experienced they are, will learn something and have fun reading this book.

The best part of this book is that it is broken into many independent sections that are short and easy to read in a few minutes. Each story is geared to be fun while still informative. This is a great book for either the coffee table or the porcelain throne, and it makes a great guide to be taken along on every outdoor journey where water wildlife is involved! It is the perfect gift for any outdoorsman!

If you are that pro fly-fishing guy or technical bass fisherman searching for some obscure secret, this is not that book! This book is for most of us regular outdoors folks, but I bet even you hard-core guys will learn something and really enjoy this book.

Even though I don't claim to be an expert in any type of fishing, the fact remains that after fishing for nearly sixty years, landing thousands of fish and other creatures and making over a thousand spear-fishing dives—along with undertaking so many other water-creature-slaying adventures that it would be impossible to count—it is hard not to accept that I am somewhat of an authority in this field. I like to say that I am "the best fisherman that has ever crapped behind two shoes," but this statement causes fierce debate among my friends and family!

    Enjoy your read, my friend!

STRIPED BASS FISHING

Author's wife with striped bass

Catching striped bass in shallow, swift water with live bait — that's true excitement!

One of the best striper fishing trips I've ever had was when a friend of mine and I were fishing some sloughs in the Sacramento Delta. The sloughs were between and amidst duck hunting clubs that were flooded from the water in the river. These ponds had floodgates on their upper end that would let the river water run into them at high tide, and when the tide went out, there were outlet pipes on the lower end to release the water back into the slough. I think these are so the water in the ponds stays fresh. The pipes on the lower end of the ponds can become exposed during low tide, especially on a minus tide or extremely low tide. Whenever the water in the river is lower than that in the ponds, the water that is in the pond, along with all of the little bugs, baitfish, crawfish, and what have you, pours out of the pipes back into the river. Where this water pours into the river, it causes a ten-foot round, five-foot deep underwater hole from the erosion and a little fifteen-foot-wide channel through the tulles to the main river channel that is only three feet or so at low tide. As you know, fish like rushing water because they feed there and it is rich with oxygen. Put a hose in any aquarium and you will see every fish migrate to where the water is flowing its fastest. Striped bass are no different.

We baited up our striper rigs with a goby, which is a little bullhead-type mudsucker that resembles a small catfish. Any live bait would work, I am sure. We would open the baitfish's mouth and put the fishhook through his upper mouth so as not to sew his mouth shut, which keeps him alive. We used no fishing weight at all, just the weight of the bait. We lifted our boat motor and pulled our boat right up in the little channel. Our cast was just a little underhanded toss into the pool right where the swirling water rushing out of the pipe was, and we let it drift naturally. Bam! We would catch two or three keeper stripers within minutes, and then we would move to the next floodgate!

Without any fishing weight and only a fishhook on the bottom of your fishing line, it is just you and your fish! Right when you set the hook, the fish will panic, and you are in for a fight in very close quarters, and that fish does not mean to get caught! Fishing so close to the boat and with such a confined body of water like this, you have no benefit from the fishing line stretching to help with the fight. Your drag is important, but because of all the close-in and fast action, using a fishing rod with a limber tip, as well as "giving and taking" the pole properly, is the key to not losing the fish. Keeping that line tight is always important with any fish, but because of the soft tissue in the striped bass's mouth, it is even more important. This is challenging when that striper is jumping violently right next to you! Giving that striper your fishing rod tip when it demands it and yanking it back in a split second as the striped bass breaks the water or darts towards you is your only hope. Boy, you talk about fun. One day, we caught and released twenty-five keeper striped bass between five and twelve pounds each. Now that is some of the best striped bass fishing I ever had.

So, keep your eye out for that flowing water and those eddies behind it. It may be from a pump station, water flowing over a weir, a narrowing of a river or other waterway, or water coming out of a creek. The fish like these spots. I like fishing sturgeon in areas like this as well. Most of the sturgeon I have ever caught have been in less than ten feet of water!

Trolling for stripers and catching them two at a time

Trolling for striped bass is an exciting way to fish. Those stripers hit hard, which feels pretty good to us fishermen. When they hit a lure being trolled at a good pace, it is like they mean to tear the fishing pole right out of the boat—every time!

Rig for catching stripers two at a time

When the stripers are running good, I have even been known to catch them two at a time. I use a fishing rig that has a Hair Raiser lure on a split ring up about three feet from the jointed-backed Rebel lure. I attach a three-way swivel to the line that goes to the fishing rod, with the three-foot leader tied to the other end that has a snap swivel at its end to attach whatever color Rebel I use. I snap the split ring directly to the third eye of the three-way swivel and Hair Raiser lure with no leader at all.

The Hair Raiser is a giant fishing jig with a large and heavy jig head on it, which acts as a weight for the entire fishing rig. The Rebel that I use is a deep-diving sort with the big spoon on the front that drives the lure downward when pulled through the river. If the water is a little shallow, I might switch to the Rebel, which has a much smaller spoon on it. It doesn't dive so much, and I run the tackle a little shallower, especially if there are a lot of snags in the area.

The striped bass like to run in schools, and sometimes you will see a second or third fish follow the one that is on the hook right up to the boat when you are getting ready to net it. Sometimes those other fish just can't resist that second lure because they think that other fish is getting all the food. So next thing you know, you have two fighting fish on the line! When they are thick, I like to set the hook and continue trolling a minute or two to tease those other fish into attacking the free lure while the rig is still amidst the school of fish. Then if nothing else hits shortly, I fight in the one I have.

I use this fishing technique when the smaller striped bass are present, but not when the larger lunkers are in the river. Then, I will often use the two lures in the same manner—but when I know I have that twenty- or thirty-pounder on there, the battle begins immediately!

When I was a kid, fifty years ago, they used to plant salmon down in the delta of the Sacramento River in Northern California so they could make it past all the predator fish as they made their way to the ocean from further up the river where they were bred in hatcheries. They would drop those fingerlings into the river, and the fish would head for the shade of docks, pilings, and other structures immediately. The stripers would have an absolute feeding frenzy! My dad and I would troll along these shady areas and catch some huge stripers, and a lot of them. We would keep our limits of the good-eating small fish and fish until we could hardly reel anymore! Boy, what a lot of fun that was, and a great way to spend a day with a good friend.

Trolling for stripers in shallow water near shore – my best striper-trolling tip

One of the best striped bass trolling tips I can share with you is to troll for stripers along the banks of rivers. Often I see people trolling for striped bass in deep water, using deep-diving Rebels, which is one way to get them because there are so many that you can find striped bass about anywhere. But trolling for striped bass near shore, and especially where there are tule clumps along the banks, has always proven to be more productive. I also like to troll for stripers near rocky banks where the levees have been riprapped and where there are willow trees and other brush hanging over the water. Minnows and other baitfish inhabit areas where they have protection from predators in such close-in areas as this, and this is where striped bass feed most often.

Don't hesitate to troll for striped bass in these shallow waters. By that, I mean water that may be two or three feet deep so your boat will barely run in it. I fish in the delta area mostly, and the area is tidal, so at low tide some of the areas that I like to troll are too shallow to run the boat until the tide comes in a couple feet. While waiting for the tide to come in, I often float out further and cast lures towards the tule and brush patches along the shore. If I am trolling for striped bass along a rocky shore where riprap was used for levee erosion control, I am often trolling so close in that I have to watch hitting my prop on some of the larger rocks. I am seldom trolling more than ten or fifteen feet from the bank.

My favorite lure to use for trolling for striped bass is the jointed-backed Rebel. The best color of lure for striper trolling is usually silver or blue or a mixture of these. A little red at the gill area on any colored lure for catching striped bass is never a bad idea. These striper lures come with a lot of options, and you need to know which one is the best striped bass trolling lure for the type of striper fishing that you are doing. There are deep-diving Rebels and shallow-water Rebels with the difference being the size and shape of the "spoon" on the front of them, which determines the amount of water they catch. When trolling near the bank for striped bass, you want a Rebel lure with a very small spoon on the front that takes the lure just under the water a foot or two. In deeper water or more open water, such as out on a big sandbar or on a mud clam bed, I like to troll for big striped bass with a long Rebel that is not jointed in the back and acts more like a huge pike, split tail, or other large baitfish. In any case, don't be afraid to use a large lure when trolling for striped bass. Their mouths are huge, and they will try to put anything in it that will fit! I have caught one-foot striped bass on five-inch gobies. My cousin likes to use live baitfish for striped bass that are no less than twelve or fifteen inches and is not afraid to use a baitfish over twenty inches. He lost a striper one time that he hooked on a twenty-seven inch split tail!

The best speed for trolling for striped bass is usually faster than most people would think. Striped bass are fast swimmers and will attack anything that they can catch. Even though your striper trolling speed is fast, if you think about it, you are still trolling much slower than what the average baitfish can swim. Any fish can dart away at lightning speed when there is a huge open mouth motivating them! Having said that, like any fish, striped bass eat what they can catch, and often an injured or slow baitfish is easy prey. These might move a little slower and be the best food for a striped bass at the time. So when you are trolling for striped bass, you may alter your speed from time to time if they aren't biting and see if you can stir up some striper action. However, you may want to move to a different area if you have made eight or ten passes and have had no luck.

Another of my best tips for trolling for striped bass is that once you catch a big striped bass, continue to fish that same area. You might want to make a loop and fish that same area immediately and in the same direction. When trolling for striped bass, you will often find them in groups or schools. After all, the best place to troll for striped bass is where they are — and never look a gift horse in the mouth! There may be a big concentration of baitfish, crawfish, a desirable current flow, or some other thing attracting striped bass to the area, along with the fact that fish like to hang out with other fish.

If you notice that there are fingerling salmon or other fish being planted, start trolling by any docks, pilings, or shade and structure in that area. The striped bass will move in immediately to take advantage of these disoriented baitfish and will feed on them in a frenzy! My dad and I used to catch them two at a time during salmon planting times when I was young. You can read about that in my other striper-trolling article.

So what are you waiting for? They are out there biting right now!

Using a bait runner reel with large, live bait – my favorite way to catch striped bass

Catching striped bass with live bait using a bait-runner reel is an exciting and effective technique. Just catching the baitfish to fish with is fun!

A gobe bait fish

First, you need to catch the bait that you plan to use. These are local fish in the waters that you are fishing in, and they can be squawfish, mudsuckers, gobies, split tail, perch, bluegill, or any other such fish that is legal to fish with. Every fisherman should check the local fishing regulations for their area, as each will have variations of what baitfish are legal. Transporting any live fish into a body of water from another area is usually not allowed. The bigger the stripers you are after, the bigger the baitfish you want to use. My cousin uses split tails over two-feet long once in a while! It's not that you can't use smaller baitfish when you are fishing for large striped bass, it's just that the smaller ones will steal your bait and you will catch those instead before the rare monster comes looking for prey.

To catch the baitfish, I like to use a fly rod. I am not good at fly-fishing, trust me. I just like to use it as a cane pole to reach around into the tules, brush, and other cover due to its length and sensitivity. Wharfs and docks are good baitfish hangouts. I use a small hook with a split shot above it about a foot or so. I like to use red worms or a piece of night crawler threaded onto the hook and up the line a bit. Dangle this fishing rig amidst the cover and move it around from time to time to try a different spot. Set lines are handy for this, which are just little four-foot pieces of fishing line with the hook and weight set up the same way. It is nice because you can be baitfishing while you are fishing. Have a bait cage that floats in the water if you can so that you can keep the baitfish alive and lively as long as possible. If you fish the same place often, it is nice to just leave the cage there and save the baitfish for the next time you fish. Anyway, catching baitfish is just like catching any fish. You will feel the bite and set the hook and there you go.

When you bait the baitfish, you will want the sharp end of the hook to be facing towards the tail of the fish and situated directly behind the top of its head. The big stripers like to attack head first, so this positions the hook for just that. You will accomplish this by using a hook threader. For the bigger baitfish, you may have to make your own that is long enough to go from the tail of the fish, under the skin, to that area right behind its head. This may be a foot or more. You will force the line up under the skin to behind the head until it protrudes out there and then tie the hook to it. Then, you will tug the line a little from the tail and push the hook's eye under the skin, leaving just the "u" shape with the point and barb visible. This will allow the baitfish to swim around forward naturally with the line invisible from the front of the fish and allow its free movement in the water. If you need to build a line threader that will work for the bigger fish, check out the smaller ones available at the tackle shops and you will get the idea.

The fishing rig setup for this type of fishing is simple. The line that you tied to the hook should be about three or four feet long. The other end will be tied to a swivel. The line coming from your fishing pole will have a sliding sinker setup threaded onto it, and it will then be tied to the other end of the swivel. Basically, this swivel serves as a "stop" to keep the sliding sinker above the leader. Snap the weight to the slide and you are done. How much weight will depend on the current, tide, and such, but you are probably talking an ounce or two. My thought is that any time you are fishing, the less weight the better, so when the fish bites on the bait it feels as natural as possible. Fish do not like to feel resistance that is un-natural; how they know this is a mystery, but they do. Same when you set the hook. They know that it ain't no accident and that they better start fighting for their lives!

The pole is important, as is how you "prop" it up, for this very same reason. A stiff fishing rod tip is resistance. I like a tip that's a little more limber but a stout pole to set the hook hard when needed. I call setting the hook "puttin' the wood to him"! When you set your pole down to fish, don't shove it into a fish holder or lean it hard against the side of the boat or the dock railing and such. Find a way to set it securely balanced so that it is on a fulcrum like a teeter-totter. This way, with your light rod tip and the pole readily and easily tilting towards the river, when you get a pull from that big striper, the resistance that the fish feels is very minimal, and he is more apt to take the bait full force without hesitation. He will usually run with it for ten or twenty feet and then stop while he turns the fish around tail first into swallowing position, and then will run full force again, which is when you PUT THE WOOD TO HIM!!!!

Allowing the fish to freely run would not be possible if it weren't for your reel being built for it. They sell the "bait running" reels for this very purpose. They have a switch that frees the line to unreel with nearly no resistance as the fish begins to run with the bait. The reel may make a slight clicking sound, and the resistance is adjustable (to slow down the big baitfish some). When the fish is on the run and it stops, or it is just running and you decide to set the hook, you will dip your rod tip towards the fish to give the line slack, reel the handle until the reel locks into place, let the fish take the slack out of the line, and then you, yes, yes, you got it—PUT THE WOOD TO HIM!!!! Hopefully, your drag is set correctly for the size of fish that you have and the size of the line you are using. I personally like eighteen-pound test line most of the time unless I am going for a little bigger fish, then twenty-five might be better. And don't use cheap line, you cheapskates out there!

Using a bobber for catching stripers

Catching striped bass with a bobber is another striped bass fishing technique that you might try. It is a simple way to catch striped bass that most folks have never tried and is a great way to catch striped bass that is exciting and relaxing. And you don't need a bunch of expensive tackle!

This striped bass fishing rig is a simple setup. It is just like bobber fishing for crappie on a bigger scale. I like to use big gobies or other live baitfish, such as split tail or pike. Typically, the bigger the bait, the bigger the fish you are apt to catch. Just make sure you bring some bigger bobbers so that your baitfish can't pull it under the water. Tie a hook on the end of the line with a three-way swivel up about two or three feet above the baitfish. Use a split ring and attach a weight that is adequate to keep your bait under the water. Hook the baitfish with a large hook under the dorsal fin.

While striped bass fishing using this technique, adjust the depth of your bait from time to time if you aren't getting any bites. Start with your weight at about eight feet down. Just toss the bobber out and wait! You can either anchor or drift along. I prefer to drift unless I am near where there is water running into the area from the tide, an irrigation pump, or some other reason. Then, I like to stay near the moving water because the fish like to come to it. The bobber will be quite active if you have a big baitfish on, and you may have to get used to it seeming like you have a bite all the time. But you will know when that big striped bass hits the baitfish because it will hit it hard and your bobber will disappear, or it will grab the fish and take off with it and drag your bobber steadily across the top of the water.

Some folks will use a bait runner reel for this striped bass fishing technique, which isn't a bad idea. But if you get hit hard, set the hook immediately because the striped bass will not like the resistance that he feels from the bobber when he hits it. Using a smaller baitfish so the big bass can take it deep into their engine room right off the bat instead of hitting it in the head to kill it and then turning it around to swallow it is not a bad idea. I personally like a six- to ten-inch baitfish for catching striped bass this way.

Fishing stripers with cut bait

Fishing for striped bass doesn't have to be expensive, complicated, or require using a boat. I grew up in the Sacramento Delta in California, and most of the striped bass that I have caught have been from shore fishing with a very simple

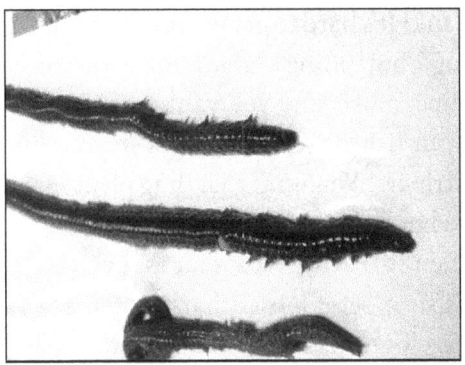

Pile Worm

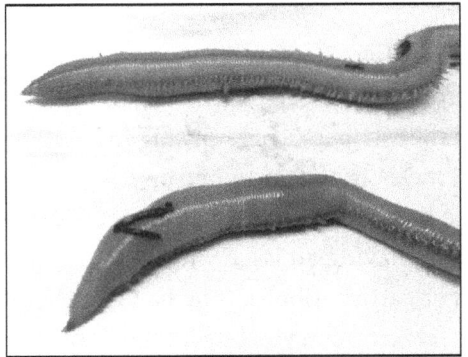

Blood Worm

fishing setup and using cut bait, such as sardines, anchovies, or shad. I also like to use pile worms and bloodworms, but they get a little pricey.

The rigging that I use for striper fishing with cut bait consists of a hook on the bottom of a three- to four- foot leader that is tied to a swivel and has a sliding sinker setup on the line above the swivel. I use enough weight that will hold the line from drifting too close to the bank in the current from the tide. I change the weight to a heavier one as needed if the water gets swifter from the tide going out or coming in. I prefer using as little weight as needed so the fish feel as little resistance as possible when they nibble. That is also why the sliding sinker rig is useful, along with "balancing" your pole like a "teeter-totter" on the pole holder. You can learn much more about this idea in the article here about fishing with a bait runner reel, and I highly recommend that you read that article, as it is much more in depth than this one and much of the fishing techniques discussed there are important when fishing with cut bait as well as fishing with live bait. Fishing with cut bait allows stripers and other fish of all sizes to nibble away on your hook, and the smell of fresh-cut sardines carries through the water to attract all types of fish, while fishing with live bait doesn't have this issue. Sometimes, fishing with live bait becomes essential to keep from constantly losing your bait to small fish.

I like to use eighteen-pound test fishing line for both the line and the fishing leader when fishing with cut bait. I use a large hook with a big bend, such as a 1-0 or so. Make sure you use a sharp hook, not one of those free ones you found rusting on the rocks of the river bank! It's hard to get too big of a hook for striped bass because their mouths are huge, but hiding a large hook with a piece of bait can be challenging. And, of course, make sure you yank on your fishing line to make sure that the drag on your fishing reel is set right so your line doesn't snap when you hook those big stripers! You want that drag plenty firm to set that hook in good if you happen to hook the striper in the hard part of its mouth, but you want it to pull freely when that striped bass takes off running with it after you hook him. If you aren't sure, set it looser than tighter, as you can always tighten the drag while you are fighting the fish if needed. A good expensive reel will have a much smoother drag and truly aid in landing big fish as compared to a cheaper model.

Cut your bait so that you get a chunk big enough to cover the hook. This might be a whole anchovy or half of a sardine. Some folks prefer to cut the heads off their baitfish, and I am sure from experience that this leads to more striper bites. It also leads to bites by smaller stripers where the big fish will be happy to swallow the head in one bite. I have cut the guts open on scads of big striped bass in my day, and those sardine heads are in there. Sardine heads stay on the hook much better as well if you are having an issue with keeping your bait on the line from small striper bites or catfish nibbles. The bait is difficult to keep on anyway because most of it is frozen when you buy it these days and becomes mushy when it is thawed. Some folks tie it on with thread or even wrap it in cheesecloth to keep it on better.

Unlike fishing with live bait, when fishing with cut bait, I like to hold my pole and set the hook on any good bite that I get. With live bait you let the fish run with it a while. When fishing with cut bait, it is usually frozen and thawed and has very little texture to cause it to stay on the hook. You only get a couple of bites and it is gone. The good thing about fishing for striped bass is that when you get a bite from a large striper, you know it! The smaller ones will nibble and nibble at your bait. The big stripers will darn near yank the pole out of your hands much of the time. Boy does that feel good!!!

So now, go get 'em!!!

ALL YOU NEED TO KNOW ABOUT STURGEON FISHING!

Author's nephew with a lunker sturgeon

Sturgeon are the pre-historic giants of all the freshwater fishes, often reaching over seven feet in length and up to several hundred pounds. A large female may carry nearly a hundred pounds of eggs alone! For that reason, most fisheries are protected by a "slot limit" that requires that both the very young and small sturgeon be released as well as those exceeding a particular length so that these valuable egg producers can proliferate. Since the adoption of these slot limits, any long-time sturgeon fisherman can attest to the fact that there are scads more sturgeon in the waters. The slot varies from area to area, so make sure you familiarize yourself with the specific rules in the area that you are fishing. As always, practicing catch and release is always a sporting and healthy practice.

Sturgeon have unique body characteristics that highly influence the tackle that is used. Sturgeon have raised ridges along their backs and on both sides that are very sharp and bone-like. The ridges are actually a series of protruding ridges and valleys, with an inch or two in distance from the peak of each ridge. It's as if these protrusions were designed to cut fishing line, and most certainly will if given the opportunity. That opportunity is created by the sturgeon on purpose when he knows he is on the line. The fish will roll and jump and twist, often as you are fighting it in, just to free itself. For this reason, using a wire leader when fishing for sturgeon is essential. The leaders sold in stores are about eighteen to twenty-four inches, typically, but I like to use one that is closer to three feet. This requires that I make my own, which is very simple and much less expensive. The parts are readily available at any good tackle shop in a sturgeon-fishing area, and one only needs to buy a pre-made one and examine it to learn how to make one.

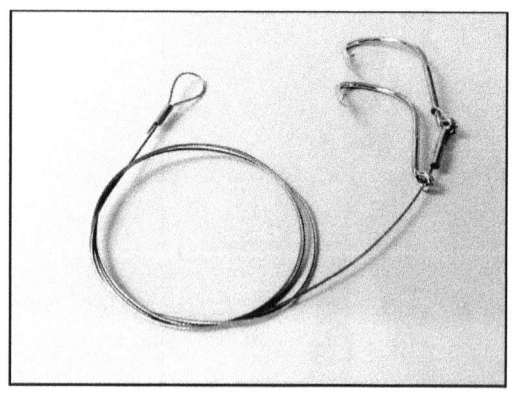

Typical wire sturgeon leader

The fishing rig for sturgeon is a simple one that consists of a "sliding sinker" setup that allows the weight to sit on the bottom and the line to pass freely through it. The weight remains above the leader and is held there by a large "barrel" swivel that has two eyes. The plastic sliding sinker rig is threaded through the line towards the fishing rod, and the swivel is then tied to the line. The wire leader, which has a heavy-duty clip on one end and the hook on the other, is attached to the second eye of the swivel. The hooks that are used are large, 4-0 or so, and are often attached so there are two of them "facing" each other. When they are taken into the sturgeon's mouth, one point and barb is pointing up and the other is pointing down, ensuring more success in hooking a fish. This double hook setup also allows for more bait to be used. Baiting two large hooks like this presents quite a "gob" of food to the fish, which I am a believer in. I prefer a good-quality, braided forty-pound test or better line for sturgeon fishing.

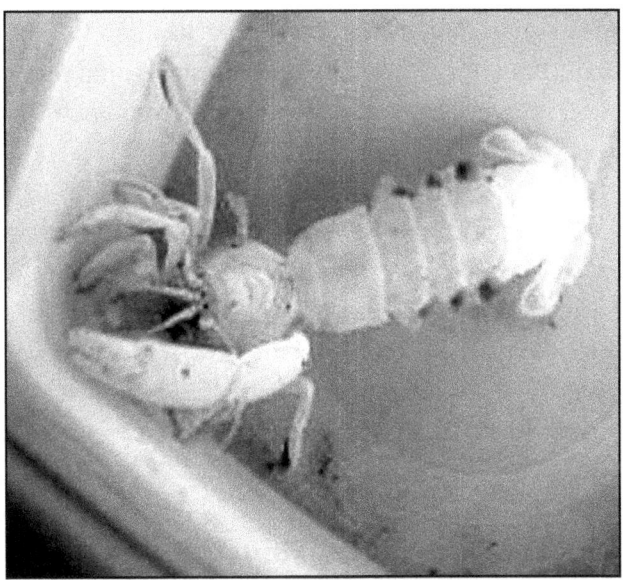

Ghost Shrimp – a favorite sturgeon bait

The bait to catch sturgeon varies. A small two-inch freshwater shrimp, called a grass shrimp, is a very popular bait. It may take twenty or more to bait the two hooks. Another bait that is very popular is ghost shrimp. These shrimp are much larger. They might be four or more inches in length and have a girth similar to your index finger. Unlike grass shrimp that are hooked on one at a time through their center and "stacked" on top of each other, the ghost shrimp are often "threaded" from the front of the head to the tail so that one or two of them will consume an entire hook. Both of these shrimp are somewhat soft-bodied and are not expected to remain on the hook through more than one bite or being freed from a snag.

A more durable bait that has become somewhat popular of late is the lamprey eel. These eel have skin like leather, and many fishermen swear by their effectiveness. I have not found this to be true, however. Although inexpensive and long lasting, this is a bait I rarely employ. When I have used it, I have baited with ghost shrimp or grass shrimp on one of the hooks and put the eel on the other, so I am certain that if a sturgeon swims by at any time, I am not fishing "naked" with no bait. Although the eel might not be my favorite bait, I am of the belief that about any hungry sturgeon will eat almost any food it comes by, and you will catch more fish with any kind of bait than no bait at all!

In some rivers, like the Columbia on the Oregon/Washington border, a popular bait is the American Shad. These fish are two to five pounds and migrate inland each year to spawn and die up the far reaches of the rivers. Many sturgeon fishermen catch these and save them for bait in the freezer. They are usually cut into hook-sized pieces and baited with the meat outward. Let me mention here that if you have never shad fished, you are missing a fantastic and exciting sport, and I recommend that you read about it here in this book for a taste of what it is like.

Other baits used for sturgeon include pile worms, small four-inch baby shad, bloodworms, anchovies, and sardines. I have not had as much success with these but have caught sturgeon on all of them. Again, hungry sturgeon aren't beggars! Also, be aware that most of the bites you might get while sturgeon fishing are not sturgeon but catfish, striped bass, and even carp. Using bait that is highly attractive to these fish, like sardines and worms, will usually inhibit your sturgeon fishing success. If you find yourself getting your sturgeon bait stolen by these other fish quickly on each cast, I advise you to move to another fishing spot.

Sturgeon have a unique mouth that has adapted over the many thousands of years that they have existed to best glean the food from where they feed. Sturgeon feed on the bottom of the waterway in the mud, gravel, and rocks found there. They scour the riprap rocks on the banks and the holes in the tules on the sides of the river. Their mouths have become the perfect tool for these activities. A sturgeon mouth is a vacuum that, when not in use, is flush with their face like any fish. However, when in use, this "rubbery" mouth will telescope outward five or even ten inches to glean the clams, shrimp, and other morsels from their hiding places.

For this reason, you will find that sturgeon bites are much different than what you would expect. When they find your bait, they often just "breathe" it in ever-so-softly. The bite is rarely a "nibble" like most fish. Most often, it is what is referred to as a "pull down." Your rod tip might slowly bend as though a piece of debris is drifting by and bumping your line, which often occurs and is often mistaken for a sturgeon bite. Usually the pull down is firm and will subside and another will follow right away. Many of my fishing buddies believe that the third such pull down is the time to yank back and set the hook, but I believe any time that you can catch the fish in the middle of the pull down is the right time. I have seen the one or two pulls without the third many a time!

As with any fish, I believe that the less resistance that the fish feels when biting, the better. I highly recommend using a "bait runner" reel that allows the line to nearly free flow from it when a fish bites, as well as mounting your pole so that it is "balancing" on a fulcrum. If you place your pole so that it "teeters," there is next to no resistance and the bites are very noticeable. However, remember to guard or secure your pole from being dragged into the water if you do hook a fish.

I want to mention a couple of other things about sturgeon bites. One is that on many occasions, not the norm but not uncommon, the fish will suck the bait in and continue swimming. Your pole will double over, and you had better have it well anchored and your drag had better be set to release line freely or your pole is going overboard—or your line, pole, or both may break. Again, using a bait-runner reel is a huge benefit.

The other thing worth mentioning is that the wind is a huge problem when sturgeon fishing. With the wind moving the boat and your rod, spotting

Author with a nice sturgeon

a sturgeon bite can be quite difficult. You are best off to find a fishing spot against a bank or structure so your boat is out of the wind.

Sturgeon live in the brackish water at the mouths of rivers where they converge with the ocean and the shrimp are abundant. In the winter and spring, they make their way up the rivers into the deeper reaches of the deltas and even up hundreds of miles into the shallows of the rivers flowing through the valleys near where the tributaries feed the main rivers. This is not to say that some sturgeon aren't in these areas nearly any time of the year, as they certainly are. But your fishing will be tenfold better during the spawning periods.

Many sturgeon fishermen think that sturgeon are found in the deepest holes in the waterway. Although they can be found in these holes, they are mostly out foraging for food on clam beds and along river banks, and many of these areas are very shallow. If I do fish a deep-hole area, I will use the depth finder to find the uphill slope facing the direction that the water is coming from. Here, some believe, is where the sturgeon swim side to side, waiting for food to wash over the hill towards them. Boats will anchor above where this slope starts so their bait drifts to a stop halfway down this underwater hill. If this hill is just below a huge tule patch or clam bed upstream, surely some food might drift in. However, I believe that hungry sturgeon are not going to sit and wait for luck but are going to get out and use their vacuum mouth and hunt their prey where it lives. For this reason, I fish mostly in the shallows on flooded islands and near levees where rocks have been placed to protect them from erosion and near tule patches or right on muddy clam beds. Most of the places that I fish are from three to fifteen feet deep, depending on the tide at the time. I have had much more success fishing in these waters than any time I have fished the deep holes. I kind of look at the deep-hole theory as a myth. I am sure the fish are there from time to time, resting from the current, but they are not feeding there regularly.

Sturgeon generally like to bite at night better that during the day. We catch a lot of them during the day, but from years of experience, I can tell you that night fishing is best. Sturgeon also prefer certain water flows. For instance, in the Sacramento Delta where I do most of my fishing, the water is tidal. It rises and lowers several feet a couple of times a day. Where we fish, ninety percent of the fish are caught in the outgoing tide and mostly during the last two hours of that tide. When the tide begins to come in, we head home. Catching the last few hours of a nice outgoing tide that happens to be at dusk is a dream time to fish. You can fish at night during prime time and still be home early enough for some TV! Many sturgeon fishermen bring a lounge chair and sleeping bag, and the "clicker" on the bait running reel is the fish-on alarm for them. Remember, too, that each area is different. My friends fish another part of the delta and find the opposite tide to be best. Over time, you will learn the best areas and times.

I want to mention water flow here. Have you ever seen what happens in an aquarium or fishpond when you put a garden hose in it to fill it? Every fish comes right to the source of the water where it is at its strongest. I believe that wild fish, including sturgeon, do the same. Except the hose is replaced with some sort of natural or man-made hydraulic action. In the delta, we have old flooded islands that fill with water at high tide, and at low tide that water gushes out into the sloughs. At high tide, it gushes inward. Fishing either side from the levee at the right time can be great. Sometimes there is an irrigation pump forcing thousands of gallons of water from the fields to the river or a weir with water pouring over it. It may just be a narrowing of the waterway that you are fishing, where the water increases in an ever-so-slight velocity that is the key. Regardless, as you are hunting for a fishing hole, keep this factor in mind.

When sturgeon fishing, you usually only check your bait if you have a bite, debris hits your line, or an hour or so has passed. Sturgeon bites are typically few and far between. Some days we might get one or two in several hours. Others, we might get ten or fifteen or zero. Two to five is probably our average, with our average fishing trip having one fish landed. However, one time my wife, nephew, and I put seventeen in the boat in two days, along with several limits of striped bass that bit our sturgeon rigs! All this in six feet of water, by the way. You have to face it: sturgeon fishing requires patience, and taking kids might not be in either of your best interests.

Catching a big sturgeon makes all the waiting and expense worthwhile! When you set that hook and feel the weight of that huge ancient dinosaur on the other end and he takes off running, making your drag sing as he strips your reel of precious line, I guarantee your heart will be pounding. When he stops and runs back at you and you are reeling at lightning speed to keep any slack from forming where he can throw the hook from his mouth any second, you will be in some of the deepest concentration of your life, and when he approaches the boat and breaks his whole body out of the water, shaking the hook and spinning to wrap your line around his razor-sharp cutting tools on his skin, you will be in absolute awe. Some people think that sturgeon just go to the bottom and tug, which could not be further from the truth. You are more apt to get that from a salmon in the river than a sturgeon.

When you do hook a sturgeon, you need to have your buddies get all the other lines out of the water immediately. If you have a rear anchor to keep the boat from swinging around in the tide, that needs to come out first and quickly, as you never know if the sturgeon is going to run at you and try to use your boat as a cutting tool on the line or what. Back in the day, when it was common to keep very large sturgeon, you would tie a float to your front anchor line with a slipknot, release your boat from it, and let the 300-pound fish drag you around until he was tired. Often you would have to fire up the motor and chase the fish to regain some of the line onto your reel that was stripped down to nearly zero in the first minutes of the battle. Now a days, it is best to just cut your line and try not to damage the huge fish or exhaust them to death, as they are the future of the fishery. One monster female may carry eighty pounds or more of roe with hundreds of thousands of eggs compared to one in the slot that has a small fraction of that.

When you do fight a sturgeon, like any fish, the more tired they are when they reach the boat, the better your odds of landing them. The less line you have out, the less the stretch and the less forgiving it is to a big run by the fish. Trust me, sturgeon and other fish clearly know that the boat means they are very close to a BBQ pit, and "second winds" are a very common occurrence!

How to clean and cook a sturgeon

Once you catch one, you will need to know how to clean it, as they are not like most other fish. Cleaning a sturgeon isn't that complicated, but it does take a little elbow grease because their hide is tough and well-adhered to their meat. You also have to be a little careful because sturgeon have sharp ridges running from head to tail on both of their sides and along their backs that can slice your hands open. Make sure you have a sharp knife on hand because a dull one will make your job much more difficult. Gloves are an excellent idea as well.

To start, lay your knife flat on the body and slice under the sharp ridges, sawing the knife back and forth for the full length of the fish to remove the entire row of ridges from head to tail, preferably in one piece. Do this for all three ridges. Then cut the skin from head to tail where these ridges once were so that the skin can be removed in three separate sections. Pulling it all off in one piece like a little catfish isn't going to happen. You may find it best to cut the skin once more from head to tail on the underside. Once the skin is sliced, you will need to grab it with pliers, or better yet, catfish skinners, and pull each section off. You might find it easier to hang the sturgeon up with a rope through its mouth and gills for this part of the cleaning process.

After the skin is off the sturgeon, slice the stomach open as for any fish and remove the innards. Save any roe inside, which is black, and get a recipe for caviar off the net and try that out. Also, sturgeon have a gizzard like a chicken, believe it or not. This gizzard has rocks and such in it, and you can slice it open to clean it. It is very good to eat. Some folks marinate it in milk and fry it, swearing it is the poor man's abalone.

Sturgeon have very few bones in them. Instead, they have a cartilage type backbone from head to tail. What bones they do have are typically found up near the head end of the body. Within the backbone is a rubbery spinal cord that must be removed. This is a little tricky because it is not something that you find yourself doing when you are cleaning fish of other varieties. This rubbery cord is tough and should be removed in one piece. You will slice the meat just above the tail of the sturgeon a couple of inches down to the cartilage. You will then snap the backbone cartilage by twisting it so the tail becomes free from the body except for the cord inside. Now, cut the head off the fish, which will sever the spinal cord up in that area. Then, just simply pull the spinal column out by pulling the tail off. This cord is very strong, and I recommend giving it to the kids to jump rope with—or you may want to spank your buddy with it while screaming, "Who's your sturgeon daddy!"

Of course, now you need to know how to cook a sturgeon. Some folks like filleting sturgeon into sections, but I like to cut it into steaks crossways. Either way is fine, but you will waste less meat cutting it into steaks. Most of the time

I marinate them in a little parsley, garlic, soy sauce, lemon juice, and white wine and BBQ them. Other times I cut them in cubes and roll them in a mixture of flour, cornmeal, breadcrumbs, and seasonings. I then deep-fry them in my Fry Daddy cooker. (I don't ever batter any fish, frog legs, or any food, for that matter, as it is too fattening and hides the flavor of the food.) I then serve them with some good tartar sauce made with scads of garlic. Another way I like it is steamed in chunks and served with pasta along with an assortment of dips, such as oyster sauce, cocktail sauce, tartar sauce, hot mustard, sesame seeds, and such, which impresses all my yuppie friends! Did I mention that I am the best cook that has ever crapped behind two shoes!

SALMON FISHING —
The Most Popular and Unusual Techniques for Slaying Them

Author's wife with nice salmon

"Long lining" – the most popular way to shore fish for salmon

This technique for casting for salmon from the bank is one of the most popular ways of fishing for salmon from the shores of rivers. It is much more common than using a flatfish lure from shore or casting with Mepps lures on gravel bars, which are explained fully in those articles in this book. Even though the latter are not as common, they also have their time and place and should not be discounted.

My friends and I have a nickname for this common type of fishing: "long lining." You will see why when this type of fishing is fully explained. Only a tuft of yarn-type material, known as a glow bug, is used for the lure for this type of salmon fishing. This method is done in swift water, usually just above where the water slows, because it falls into a deeper hole so that at the end of your drift your salmon fishing setup is just entering the head of this slow water. This is a constant casting and retrieval type of fishing, so when your tackle enters this slower pool at the end of the drift, you will immediately reel in and re-cast. Again, this is a very effective salmon angling method, and my buddy and I have gone out and caught three or four in a morning, which is pretty good action for any day of salmon fishing.

The tackle for salmon fishing with this method is relatively simple. Much of the salmon rigging can be done at home while you are watching *Honey Boo-Boo* or your other favorite TV show! Start with a three-way swivel. One eye will be used for the weight, one eye for the line to the pole, and the last for the line to the hook and glow bug fly. On the eye used for the weight, you will be using a lead "pencil" weight, which is a long, slender piece of lead about as round as a pencil covered by a cloth-type material. You will be putting a piece of surgical tubing on the swivel that will be used to hold the pencil weight once you determine how long of a piece you need for the particular swiftness of the honey hole you are fishing. Some waters are swifter or deeper and require more weight to get your salmon rig to the bottom, which is where the fish are. You will slip one end of the rubber surgical tubing over the eye of the swivel and tightly wrap it with heavy thread to firmly attach it by "pinching" it with the thread above the wide eyelet. On the eye that goes to the hook, you will be using a long leader, at least six or eight feet long, and some folks use even twelve to fifteen feet and then the hook with the glow bug. I will explain why such a long leader is desirable next, but I just wanted to add that you should have a piece of wood or some device to wrap these long leaders around to prevent them from getting tangled in your vest or tackle box if you pre-make them.

The long leader for this salmon-fishing method is essential, and the longer the leader, the more success you will have, and here is why. The salmon "pool up" in the heads of these slower water eddies to rest on their way up the river to spawn. Picture in your head eight or ten salmon facing upstream in a school, somewhat stationary, right where the swift water enters the hole. Salmon typically have their mouths open from wide to not-so-wide (but open) when they are sitting like this. As your line drifts sideways into and across this school, your light leader (ten or twelve pounds or less if you want) enters the salmon's mouth and the hook may be several feet beyond them. As the current drifts your setup, the line passes through their mouths gently until the hook enters their mouth and stops. This is when you "put the wood to him with gusto" and set the hook with all your might! The long leader has the benefit of sweeping a wider path through the water, covering much more area and greatly increasing your odds of threading your line into an open salmon mouth!

Now, this is my opinion and I have argued with many a fellow salmon fisherman about this philosophy because many think that the salmon is grabbing the glow bug that resembles a salmon egg to protect it or to kill it because it is a predator egg. Salmon do not eat when they enter the freshwater system to spawn, so we know that it isn't due to hunger. What I do know is that the longer the leader, the more success you have, which I believe supports my contention fully. Using a shorter leader is often necessary when you find yourself "combat" fishing elbow to elbow with a bunch of fellow fishermen. You can't be subjecting them to the danger of flinging around a "long line" or tangling everyone up in your rig every cast. I have seen many a fistfight and one stabbing at one popular combat fishing site!

Typical Glo-bugs for catching salmon

I don't fish for salmon in these shoulder-to-shoulder spots anymore because they have become even more crowded. These spots are popular because they are absolutely overrun with fish due to the swift water. Water flowing over weirs or dams or any hydraulic action that causes swift water is great, as salmon and all fish like this action and aeration. I striper fish in swift shallow water sometimes in the delta and it too is great. Put a hose in an aquarium and every fish, no matter what type, will come to the hose and love it! A good non-combat spot is a shallow gravel bar in a narrow strait of the river that dumps into a deeper pool that you can access by car or boat. With a boat, folks usually back-troll or jig for salmon, but this salmon fishing method is still a viable and fun way to catch salmon while anchored in the shallows at the head of a pool in your boat.

To fish, just wade out and position yourself so at the end of the drift on each cast, your line is drifting crossways into the prime part of the head of the hole. You may want to move upstream or down because you don't really know what the dynamics of the water flow are or the shape of the river bottom, so play with it. Cast upstream and try to get your drift as natural as possible, much like you would when you are fishing for wild trout in a stream. The bait entering the honey hole flowing along near the bottom as if it wasn't attached to your pole or weighted at all is perfect. Adjust the length of your pencil weight accordingly so once in a while your setup taps the bottom and you know it is where the fish are, but not dragging or hitting too often. You might reel very slowly to prevent hitting the bottom too often. If you feel any hesitation in it, set the hook with gusto, as this hesitation—as though the line has temporarily caught on the bottom—is what the typical bite feels like. When you hook up, you will know it, and you will have one of the most fun and challenging fights of your life in front of you! Having a buddy with a net downstream comes it real handy, trust me. The salmon aren't quite as fresh as those in the ocean, but many are still silver and barbeque perfectly, and the older ones make for some great smoked salmon!

Lure fishing from shore – an unusual but effective method

This is an unusual and interesting way to catch salmon from shore. Catching salmon with lures from the shore of rivers this way is truly challenging and lets you prove just what kind of fisherman you are! The tackle for shore fishing salmon with this method is inexpensive and simple. All you use is a swivel and a Mepps #5 gold lure with red beads and no weight. When you hook up with a salmon with only this tackle, it is just you and the fish! When you catch salmon in the river from the shore, they must be landed in shallow water, and any fish, especially salmon, do not like being dragged into shallow water because they know they are then one step away from a barbeque grill!

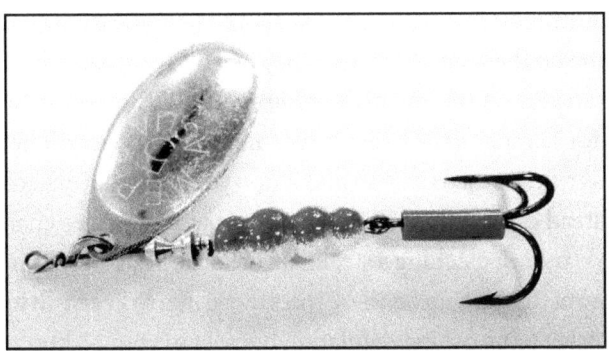

Mepps #5 Lures – My favorite salmon lure when fishing from shore

There are basically two ways to fish with a Mepps lure to catch salmon from the bank that we will talk about here. We also get them with flat fish lures a third way, which doesn't involve casting, but that is discussed in another article in this book.

The first way we catch salmon with a lure from the shore is pretty common, and the second way I have only seen done by my friends and I. The place you choose to fish is the same for either method. When you are fishing for salmon from the bank of a river, the water is usually shallow, gravelly, and there are a lot of trees and snags in the area. The river is usually meandering back and forth with many sweeping bends that have a shallow gravel bar protruding out on one side that deepens gradually as you wade out, and a steeper banked side on the other side of the river where the majority of the water flows. In between the meanders, there is often a straight channel that often narrows and gets swifter from this narrowing. Choosing where to catch salmon from the bank is a decision that involves studying these features and testing them for snags. Regardless of how good a place looks for shore fishing salmon, if there are submerged snags that will cause you to lose your fishing lure every few casts, you have to find somewhere else. Many times we would fish all day without losing a lure and would only end up changing it because the color was worn off of the body by hitting the rocks on the bottom of the river. The lures aren't cheap, but if you find something about fishing that is cheap anymore, let me know! I just went broke last weekend buying ghost shrimp and grass shrimp for sturgeon fishing.

Fishing for salmon in rivers from the shore is pointless if you are not fishing when they come up the river to spawn. They live in the ocean and are in the rivers every three or so years at the end of their life cycle to make babies, and you usually fish the rivers for salmon in the late summer and fall of the year. There is also a season and various rules in each river, so make sure you aren't the one who catches that $1500 fine instead of a salmon! Be aware, too, that these rules change often! You might also find yourself catching a steelhead or striped bass from time to time, too, so you might want to brush up on these rules if you like to keep fish to eat. Matter of fact, always just keep the fishing regulation booklet in your pickup and boat!

When choosing a place to fish salmon with a Mepps lure, you want to get on the deeper side of the bend or on a straight stretch where the river narrows so the salmon that are swimming upstream are corralled into a smaller area. Using the first method, we cast the #5 gold Mepps lure upstream at about ten o'clock and let it sink for a second or two. The river is usually only about five to ten feet deep in these areas, and the salmon are on the bottom. Then you reel the lure slowly to keep it near the bottom and spinning properly. Your lure will drift downstream to four or five o'clock as you are reeling it in because the water is swift. When the salmon hits it, you will know it, and the battle is on!

The second way of fishing with these lures is similar to the first but is kind of off the wall. We have found this method of fishing salmon from the bank of the rivers very effective if you can find the right place to do it. With this method, you cast the lure out at about ten o'clock and let it sink to the bottom. You then let the lure just "roll" along the bottom of the river on the gravel along the full distance of the area that you are fishing and you walk the bank of the river the same speed as your lure is rolling so there is no resistance by your pole that causes the lure to be drug in towards the bank. You might walk the bank of the river for a hundred yards before there are snags or the gravel bar begins to turn to a riparian forest or the bank gets too steep to walk. The salmon may bite a little differently using this technique. They may pick the lure up more softly than you expect, and you'll feel a small bite, but more often than not, they hit it with gusto. Either way, it is just you and the fish, and it is truly exciting and challenging! You have to be patient anytime you are shore fishing salmon in the river because they are not eating but attacking prey. Some days we would catch the big zip, but some days we would catch three or four!

Or you can go home and watch your favorite soap opera instead of fish!

A tricky way to fish a flatfish from shore

Fishing for salmon from shore in the rivers using the most popular lure, the Kwikfish or Flatfish, can be tough due to the swift water where this type of salmon fishing is usually done. The swift water washes your tackle too close to the shore where the salmon are less apt to run. Not to say that you have to be far from the riverbanks to catch salmon, but you still need to be in the slightly deeper and swifter main flow for success. For instance, where you typically fish for salmon in the upper stretches of the rivers, the rivers are winding and have gravel or rock bottoms. The river, as it meanders over the year, carves channels in its bottom that carry much of the water. On a long straight stretch of the river, that main channel may be anywhere within the river, but as the river meanders and bends, that main channel is usually on the side opposite the direction of the turn. This makes sense if you think about it because the main river flow is pushed to that side – it really wants to just go straight in the direction that it is traveling. This is the side that the shore fisherman should fish when using these types of lures, as the salmon typically swim in these channels no matter where these channels are in the river. Often, these channels are only twenty or thirty feet from the shore, which is very accessible to the shore fisherman using this salmon fishing method.

Typical Kwik-fish lures used for salmon fishing

The Flatfish and Kwikfish are almost identical lures with their main difference being their brand name and cost. These are large lures that have a flat front to them; in the current, they rapidly wobble from side to side. Being in the current is essential for them to operate properly and actually attract salmon, and this current must be pretty swift to do so. These lures, by design, catch a lot of the current's flow, which pushes hard on it and makes it want to wash downstream. It takes a lot of weight to hold it in place in the center of the channel that you are fishing. Matter of fact, the amount of weight is so large that casting it with a salmon fishing rod is impossible. So, how do you get it out there along with this flat fish lure? That is pretty much the subject of this article, and a great trick I learned from some old guy who is no longer with us.

To begin, you have to rig your fishing rod up correctly and realize that your lure is not going to be casted at the same time as the fishing weight, but later after it settles into the river bottom slightly downstream from where it enters the water. You are going to attach your fishing weight to a snap swivel at the bottom of your fishing leader, which should be about three or four feet long. This leader will be tied to a large eye swivel at the other end, and then the line from the fishing rod should be tied to the other end of that swivel. That is it, and the rig is set for the cast—if you want to call it that. I say that because you aren't going to cast the pole at all. You are going to throw the heavy weight out into the river as hard as you can with your hand! You are going to open the bale or unlatch the spool of your reel so that it is free to spool out as easily as possible, and make sure your pole is firmly attached to something so if you throw the weight and the line gets a backlash, your pole doesn't follow the weight right into the water! Trust me, I have seen it happen, which was an extremely humorous event to my friends and not so funny to me because it was my rod! It is best if one of your fishing buddies holds it while you throw the weight out.

The weight will drift downstream in the current until it settles. Obviously, you want to make sure that there are no snags in the area, and if you do get snagged, find another place to fish because this fishing equipment is expensive and that sunken tree trunk isn't going away soon.

The next step is to tie a snap swivel onto both ends of a three- or four-foot leader. Snap one end to your lure and snap the other end over your line near the rod tip and gently toss the lure into the current of the river. It will immediately begin to wobble and be taken downstream by the current, guided by the line that is attached to the weight. It will need a little help in its travels, especially at first, until it becomes completely submerged and starts scooping the water and working as it is made to do. To do this, you gently, but firmly, begin tapping the top of your rod tip over and over until this occurs. It will continue down the line until the snap swivel that you tied to the leader meets the eye swivel you tied above the weight, which acts as a stop. So make sure you size these two pieces of tackle accordingly. It is common for your rig to drift a little because the lure settles into place, as it is grabbing more current than the weight alone. Now you are fishing!

Fishing from the shore for salmon is not anywhere near as productive as using a boat, but it is still fun and relaxing. In a boat you can move to deep holes that salmon school and rest in and back drift your lure into them. You are going to the fish, whereas using this salmon fishing method, the fish must make it to you and the wait can be long. If you have a boat, there is an excellent article in this book on back trolling this way.

My nephew, brother, and I would sit on the gravel bar with our poles out for many hours, patiently waiting for a hit. You would know the hit because instead of your rod tip gently bouncing from the action of the lure, it would double over and almost get dragged into the river! Now, at that point with the three of us, a full-on brawl ensued no matter whose pole had the fish. We would trip, tackle, and crawl over the other to get a hold on the pole first! No telling how many fish we lost while this full-blown melee was taking place! The losers had net duty, and you better have one with you.

One time we had a huge salmon right up to the bank and fully worn out. My brother won the brawl, so he had the pole and I had the net. My dad was just watching. We all were hovered over the fish and, as my brother pulled the fish towards the bank for the final netting, we all watched the knot that I tied unravel from the lure and the fish swim off. My brother just looked up and said, "My attorneys will be in touch with your attorneys later today"! I have lived with that knot-tying incident ever since.

Back trolling – the most effective way to catch salmon from a boat

Back trolling for salmon is one of the most popular ways to salmon fish from a boat. Back trolling for salmon in rivers from a boat allows you to move from hole to hole and take the lure to the salmon, rather than sitting in one spot and waiting for the salmon to swim by your lure. The best lure for back trolling for salmon is a silver Kwikfish or Flatfish, which are also good for fishing salmon from the shore. They are pretty much the same lure and have the same action. Many fishermen swear by using a sardine wrap on the lure when back trolling for salmon. Some recommend spraying your lure with WD40 lubricant, and lately, some folks are adamant about putting a crawfish scent on a salmon lure. Regardless, learning how to back troll for salmon is important if you plan to fish rivers for salmon, and this article will give you some good tips on back trolling, the tackle for back trolling, and how to rig for back trolling.

Back trolling for salmon is a salmon fishing method used for fishing for salmon in rivers where the water is not tidal and is usually somewhat shallow and relatively swift. For instance, the faster-flowing parts of the water might be between three and fifteen feet deep and occasionally it will flow into a little deeper "pool," or it might flow through a narrow and swift channel and drop into a wider and deeper spot where the water slows, which is where the salmon tend to rest and "hold." In effect, you will be "backing" your lure into these resting spots right on the bottom of the river and presenting your lure to those salmon in that hole. You might pull the boat up after fishing that hole to above that hole again six or eight times, and then move to the next hole up or down the river. Watching where other boats, especially guides, are back trolling for salmon is a good way to find good places to back troll on your next trip or later in the day after that hole has had time to "rest." Just observing the river's flow and knowing that you are looking for these resting spots is enough to allow you to have a great fishing day, as you will recognize these resting spots. Keep your eye out for "snags" in these holes because your tackle is expensive. Sometimes you can actually see the snag in the water, and other times you can see a "bump," swirl, or some other irregularity in the water indicating a snag. If by chance you do lose some tackle to a snag, find a different hole or at least stay away from that snag in that hole. Again, you will be putting your lure in upstream in the swift channel and "backing" it into these holes. It is good to note that there is usually a "channel" that is a little deeper in these swift portions of the river, which are identifiable with your depth finder, and backing your lure in where these run into the pool is a good thing, but coming into the hole in different areas is a good idea because most of the rivers you are fishing will be pretty good sized.

Rigging for back trolling for salmon is a simple task. First, you need to understand how the Kwikfish or Flatfish work and interact with the water so you can easily get the idea of the rigging. These lures have a big flat "head," and the eye that attaches to the swivel on your leader is on top of this flat head. The lure points down and grabs the water with gusto. This causes the lure to move violently from side to side in a somewhat consistent manner. For this lure to work properly, there must be a fair amount of water flow past it (resistance) or it will have very little action and will not be attractive to the fish. I explain this because you are going to be "backing" this lure into the hole, and if you back it too rapidly and its speed comes closer to matching the speed of the river, you will lose the action of the lure and be wasting your time. These lures "grab" a lot of water and pull hard against your pole, so you do have some leeway to let it drift backwards and still have plenty of action to the lure. You also need to know that the salmon are on the bottom in these holes, for the most part. It is believed that they attack these lures to "kill" them because they recognize them as predator fish to their eggs and offspring. Salmon do not eat once they enter the river system from the ocean to spawn far upstream in the river and its tributary creeks. So you want to have good action and enough weight to keep the lure on the bottom, but not so much weight that your lure will not move downstream freely when you allow your boat to back towards the hole. You will find yourself lifting the weight with your pole a little as you move along backwards so it dislodges from the gravel bottom and drifts along a little from the current, and then do this again and again throughout the drift.

Back to the tackle for back trolling salmon. Basically, you will be using a three-way swivel at the end of the line to the pole, with a short "drop" line to the weight, and then the leader to the lure. I usually use about a seventeen-pound test line and the same for the leader or sometimes a little lighter leader. The leader is about three feet long with a barrel swivel on each end, one for the Flatfish and one that will be attached to one eye of the three-way swivel. The "drop" line to the weight should be about a foot and can be tied directly to the three-way swivel, but I recommend using a swivel to attach the weight, as this weight moves a lot on the rocks and the knot will take quite a bit of abuse.

Of course, the line from the pole will be attached to the last of the three eyes on the three-way swivel. The weight will probably be only about three or four ounces, but you can adjust it for the flow of the river so you get that desired "bounce" along the bottom. I use a silver lure, usually, and sometimes one with that metallic blue hue on it. These are also very large flatfish – probably the biggest you will find in the tackle shop and especially made for salmon fishing. The tackle folks can certainly help you with this decision.

A huge part of learning how to back troll for salmon is learning how to back the boat for backtrolling. This is of the utmost importance because this is what keeps the lure with enough resistance against the current so that it works properly. You have to use a motor, or oars if you are using a drift boat, to maintain that perfect speed backwards along through the swift channel and into and through the hole you are fishing. Your pole tips should be bobbing up and down in a jerking motion, very violently and consistently as it grabs and releases that water on its flat head. If this is not happening, you are drifting too fast with the current (or you may have weeds or debris on your lure), and you need to correct this. You will get the hang of this feeling with time and learn to recognize a properly working lure's action on your pole.

Now, there are spinners for backtrolling that folks use as well as roe. I personally like using Flatfish or Kwikfish, as they are consistently the best lures for backtrolling for salmon and usually as productive as any other bait or lure. Many folks swear that it is important to "tune" your lure by turning its eye where the leader line attaches one way or the other so the lure does not tend to travel to one side or the other when you put it in the swift water. You can insert the lure next to the boat with the tip of the pole, observe it, and then turn the eye until it runs "true." You may as well do this because it takes minutes and it very well may improve your fishing success.

TROUT AND STEELHEAD

Author and friends with some nice trout

Catching steelhead from shore in swift water

Fishing in rivers during the first fall storms is the best time to catch steelhead in the rivers. Catching steelhead from the banks of a river is dangerous, as the best water flow for catching steelhead is just after a storm that "blows out" the river into an unfishable rage and when the water level falls and just begins to clear of the mud but before it clears to the point where the steelhead can see you on the shore. The best time to catch steelhead is early in the morning so that you are climbing down mossy rocks and ledges in the dark to get to your best steelhead fishing spots, with the water raging below in a pool at thirty or forty miles an hour and then surging into whitewater where survival if you fall in is unusual. But the hardcore steelhead anglers find it worth the risk!

The tackle for steelhead fishing in rivers is relatively simple. The best tackle for steelhead fishing is a glow bug on an eighteen-inch leader to a small three-way swivel where a weight is attached or a small swivel with an egg sinker above it on the line. I prefer a twelve- to eighteen-pound test fishing line, depending on the swiftness of the water. If a twelve-pound steelhead turns sideways and catches the current, you need all you can get! If he darts downstream into the whitewater rapids, regardless of what line you are using, you are pretty well screwed unless he decides to head back in your direction.

When casting glow bugs for steelhead, your drift is much like any type of trout fishing. You want the drift to be natural and float more towards the bottom. The best weight to use when steelhead fishing depends on the speed of the water flow and the depth of the pool you are fishing. You may find yourself using from just over an ounce to a half ounce or less to get just the right natural drift. Also, when casting glow bugs for steelhead, you have to cast upstream and take up the slack, but not pull your line with your pole so that when your line gets in front of you to downstream at about the four to five o'clock position, the glow bug is drifting in the current naturally like it was floating from upstream, like any salmon egg or creature would. The slightest unnatural resistance caused by you or too much weight will all but kill your chance at having success at hooking a steelhead. There is a good article that expands on the drift and fishing in this manner in this book that you should read whether you are trout fishing in a stream or steelhead fishing in a swift river.

Catching steelhead in swift water is a real challenge. Setting your drag is of the utmost importance. Many times when fishing, you can set your drag looser than you might need just to err on the side of caution. When steelhead fishing, you need to have that drag set hard enough to set the hook in their hard "steel" heads and to horse them a little from wanting to take off freely downstream, but loose enough so when the steelhead darts like lightning on a run that your line doesn't break. Using a nice long eight- or nine-foot pole made just for steelhead fishing is also a big part of the equation. Steelhead mean business when they are hooked, and they have both the physique and the swift water to give them the advantage over you and your equipment, no matter how good a steelhead fisherman you think you are. Plan on losing a lot of fish and a good amount of tackle as far as that goes! It is just part of the game when fishing steelhead in swift rivers like this.

When fishing for steelhead from the bank, you often find yourself among other fishermen in a "shoulder to shoulder" situation. As a whole, steelhead fishermen take their sport more seriously than other types of fishermen and can be quite uptight and impatient with the newbies. Make sure you cast in order so you don't tangle with them and announce your movement if you are coming and going behind them so they don't snag you. Often, you are fishing on a ledge with death assured if you fall in, so make sure you move carefully and do not bump into anyone. I also strongly suggest wearing a life vest so at least they can find your body! It could also save your life.

Steelhead fishing in a drift boat is a great way to catch steelhead and much more to my liking as I get older. This too can be dangerous, and rowing in the swift water takes experience and knowledge. I strongly suggest that the average person hire a professional steelhead fishing guide service so you can learn the best tackle for steelhead fishing as well as have a safe and successful steelhead-fishing trip.

Once you find some steelhead fishing rivers that you like, you will learn that they all have gauges that show the river levels and flows. Most have recorded messages and are posted online so that you can judge when the best time to fish for steelhead will be after a storm ends. You will learn that when the gauge is reaching a certain level that you should drop everything and take off so you are there at the best time to catch steelhead. The window where steelhead fishing is the best is just a couple of days, and then the river level drops and the water clears up and they become cagy and stop biting. You should also watch the weather because even if the water level is approaching the best flow for steelhead fishing, if a storm is setting in the water will take a sudden rise and your trip will be wasted. You need that little break between storms. If you like challenging fishing, this sport is definitely one for you to try no matter how far you have to travel!

The ever-important trout "drift"

Whether you are drifting bait, such as a worm, cricket, or salmon egg, or an artificial fly while fly-fishing, the key component to success is the same: drifting the bait correctly. Those big trout didn't get that way from being stupid, and their feeding habits are well ingrained. Simply put, the proper drift is just making the bait or fly drift naturally, as it would if it were a bug or worm that fell into the water upstream by accident. This is trickier than it sounds because you have the dynamics of the fishing line being attached to a fixed point (your pole) along with the requirement that you have enough weight to cast the bait far enough into the stream. Also, the line lying in the creek is swept around, causing further issues, all of which can and must be overcome to allow the most successful fishing experience.

The most important factor in making your cast count by obtaining the correct drift is the placement of the bait in the water when you cast. By that, I mean upstream from where you have identified a particular place in the creek that you believe might hold a fish such that when the bait reaches that location, it appears natural as food floating freely. This requires that you cast upstream far enough above that site to let the bait adjust in the water to meet that goal. You will be using your pole to position your line for the cast to allow the float to be natural and to a point where you can use it to set the hook in the fish when needed. For instance, you would flip your line when fly-fishing so as to place the line upstream from the fly so the fly is presented to the fish, not the line. If bait casting, you want to take up some slack in the very beginning of the drift so you can watch your line go by in front of you without too much slack. In either case, you want the line to begin floating naturally in the water far above your target location so that the whole presentation becomes "one with the creek" by the time it gets there. Every creek is different, as are the feeding habits of different trout in different waters and at different times of day, but a general rule of thumb to start with is to cast upstream at ten o'clock as a starting point. Casting much further makes it hard to address the slack that is created and leads to snags on the bottom and also ruins the drift because the bait or line can drag on the bottom, causing the bait to stop in the creek, which is truly unnatural and not enticing to the trout. And remember to identify a particular place in the brook that you want to fish on each and every cast, or you are just randomly floating and hoping for the best. Floating your bait over and over in the same drift is rarely productive, as is not moving along in the creek and just fishing the same spot like you would when catfishing. When you do move along, remember that to get a proper drift to a particular spot, such as an eddy behind a rock, you may only move a few feet at a time. Study the creek and fish it all. Don't rush and fish each place that looks like it might hold a fish until you are convinced that you have properly presented your bait to it a couple of times. Then move to the next eddy, riffle, or slow spot. That is the fun and relaxation of it all!

Weighting your bait with whatever type of weight, if any, is also a key issue. If the stream is a raging whitewater and you are fishing a pool amongst it, like much steelhead fishing is, you might be using a half ounce or more of weight to get it down near the bottom, as though the bait was coming from a mile upstream. Fishing a typical mountain stream after the rush of snowmelt has passed might be done with simply the weight of the bait itself, using very light line and tackle, which is the best-case scenario. Everything else is in between. When you see an angler using a heavy pole and/or heavy line, you are looking at the recipe for failure!

Catching wild trout in streams

Catching wild trout is nothing like catching planted trout. Fishing for wild trout requires patience; you stalk them as if you are hunting. Unlike planted trout, fishing for wild trout requires that you move slowly and sneak up on them. If a wild trout sees you or feels you tromping on the ground and talking, your wild trout fishing trips will never be successful.

You can identify good wild trout streams by checking with your local fly shop or bait shop along with reading the fish and game regulations for your area. Often the streams that contain wild trout have special regulations, such as the requirement for using an artificial lure with only one single barbless hook on it in order to preserve the wild trout population. Most wild trout fishermen practice catch and release. If I do eat wild trout, it is usually wrapped in tin foil and cooked right when caught over a small campfire on the side of the creek as a one-time annual ritual. I practice catch and release when fishing for wild trout, and I strongly encourage all those who angle for wild trout to do the same to preserve the sport for your grandchildren and generations beyond.

Many of the best wild trout streams are found in areas that are remote and difficult to access. One wild trout stream that I fish is a three-hour hike through wilderness area along the Pacific Crest Trail in the Sierra Nevada Mountains in Northern California. The creek is very small and has shallow pools and rapids. The creek bank is washed nearly bare in many spots from the raging snow melt in the spring but slows to a small babbling brook in the summer when the season opens in that area in late May. In many spots this creek is only a few inches deep because it is wide for the amount of water that is in it, and the trout can see you coming a mile away, and if they do, that fishing hole is ruined for the day!

Another of my favorite and best wild trout fishing streams is a mountain meadow that has a small creek meandering through it for a couple of miles. It is a very marshy and wet area, and the creek is dammed in many places with beaver dams that divide the creek into two or three smaller creeks. There are places that are almost unfishable due to the canopy of small willow trees hanging over and into the brook. Many places the creek is so narrow that you can jump over it and tall meadow grasses line the banks, which are undercut by the current and become homes to many huge wild trout, as do the willow protected areas. There are fallen logs in the creek that have caught other floating branches and formed nearly unfishable wild trout habitat. All of these nearly impossible places to fish are where the big wild trout live and are exactly where you want to fish.

Fishing for wild trout in meadows is my favorite type of wild trout fishing. It is such a beautiful place to be, especially if you are fishing at the best time to catch wild trout, which is either at the butt crack of dawn or even better, near sunset in the evening after the sun has disappeared over the mountains and left the creek shaded. This is when you can see the trout delicately "ringing" the water ahead and advertising their presence. You will see an ever-so-delicate ring in the water from the lips of a trout softly nipping a mayfly or other bug from the creek, never guessing that behind those lips is a six-pound German brown trout that only a moment ago ate a three-inch meadow mouse that fell from the bank to its demise! There is usually a brisk mountain breeze that kicks up every evening as though its very purpose is to thwart your casting success and guard its wards from the likes of you. You look around and see a pair of foxes out for the night, appearing over and over above the high meadow grass for brief seconds as they jump in the air while frolicking with each other as their night of hunting begins. There is an eerie quietness in the air that puts you on edge and triggers a keen alertness and awareness that there is almost certainly a mountain lion crouched and wondering about you in several ways. You know you are the only one fishing here this day, and if that were not the case you would be looking for somewhere else to fish, as a mountain meadow wild trout stream only allows one visit by a man or woman for fishing on any one day and then shuts its doors like a tired shopkeeper at the end of a cold unbusy day. You only fish one direction and fish until dark, and then walk back to your car, which seemed like such a short distance as your fished your way away from it but now seems, and often is, miles away as you beeline back to it as the mountain blackness sets in.

Fishing for wild trout in meadows is a great place for fly-fishing. You have the openness for casting in many places, other than the high grass you have to avoid. The wind is another challenge because it catches your line and blows it in a loop as well as influences where the fly is presented in the water. Hitting a little three-foot wide section of the creek that has waist high grass on the sides of it is hard enough. Even the lure fishermen have difficulty placing their lure and positioning the line so it avoids the weeds. After all, if you snag your line and have to walk ahead to the creek to retrieve it, that fishing hole is ruined. And keep in mind that when fishing for wild trout you have to cast from as far away as possible to avoid detection from these wily fish that are always on guard for you and other intruders trying to fool them.

When fishing for wild trout, you have to be sly and sneak up on their lairs. One splash, clomp of the foot, cough, word, fast movement, or any other avoidable action will alert them of your presence, and it is over. This is especially true when fishing for big wild trout because they didn't get that way from being stupid and not paying attention to their surroundings. Most of them are as keen and intelligent as many of the fishermen that pursue them. Whether you are fishing a meadow for wild trout or stream fishing for wild trout where the water is more rapid and flowing, stealth is a must. You must move slowly and easily, and you may find yourself ducking or crawling as you walk to avoid detection.

The best bait for catching wild trout depends on what they are naturally eating at that particular time. The fly fisherman might visit the creek the day before and examine the current hatch of insects or other wild trout food that is presenting itself. Some foods are present and are eaten by the wild trout year round, such as worms or even meadow mice, in some cases. It depends on where you are and the size of wild trout that you are fishing for. As far as lures go, a one-eighth-ounce Panther Martin is always a good choice, and there is an article in this section about the best lures to use for trout and how to use them that you should read. When using a lure for catching wild trout, it is best to remove the treble hook and replace it with a single barbless hook or at least smash the barbs of the treble hook with pliers so the fish can be safely released without harming them more than necessary.

When fishing for wild trout, you will find the direction that you fish will be determined by the flow of the water and other characteristics of the creek. When I am lure fishing for wild trout in open water, such as flowing streams where there are rapids and pools, I often like to cast upstream and reel downstream. Sometimes this is impossible due to the swiftness of the creek where the lure is washed faster than I can reel, or the creek is too shallow and slow and the lure will fall to the bottom and snag in the rocks. Here, you have to fish across the creek or cast downstream. When fly fishing for wild trout or using bait to fish for wild trout, if you can get the right positioning on the side of the creek for casting so the bait floats by your position naturally and you can do so without being seen or heard, this is always best. But sometimes you have to fish in a less-than-perfect setting and cast upstream or down. Regardless, presenting the bait as naturally as possible is still highly important.

When fishing for wild trout in streams that are covered in willows or brush, or if the creek is small and the casting space is limited, you might find yourself dropping the bait in the water and feeding your line to the water from your hand, not from your reel and pole, so you can get as natural a drift as possible. You will feed the line so the bait flows naturally down the creek and under the willow branches or into the little quiet pool and you had better be ready for the strike. You will find this an awkward position because you may be setting the hook with your bare hand until you can find a way to engage the pole. Using the pole to feed the line is best, of course, but often the resistance of the line dragging across the eyelets kills the presentation of a natural drift. When wild trout fishing, the drift is of the utmost importance in presenting your bait to the fish, so make sure you read the article in this section on "the drift" and presenting your bait, as this is of the utmost importance for any type of trout fishing.

Catching planted trout in streams

Catching stocked trout is much different than catching wild trout. Knowing how to catch planted trout and the best bait for catching them are handy things to know, given that the majority of streams in some areas are stocked with planted trout.

Catching stocked trout is easy and requires minimal equipment. It is best to use a lightweight fishing pole along with light line. I like to use four- to six-pound test. The best bait for catching stocked trout is usually salmon eggs or power bait. Only use Pautzke red salmon eggs even though the others are cheaper. Don't ask me why, but you will catch ten times more planter trout on Pautzkes than any other salmon eggs. Do not make that mistake! As far as power bait, I like to use either the lime green with sparkles or the rainbow color with sparkles. I use a little larger hook for catching planted trout than many fishermen do. I will use a size six hook where many folks use a very little hook. Planted trout are usually pretty good sized, and using a slightly larger hook makes it easier to hook them and allows you to use more bait, making it easier to cast with no weight, which leads to a more natural drift.

When fishing for stocked trout in a stream, I usually don't use split shot or any weight so my drift is natural. Even though these are planted trout, by nature they like to see their food presented somewhat naturally. Every trout fisherman should read the section that explains how important bait presentation is and all about the "drift," whether you plan to fish for wild trout or planters. Using light fishing line allows my bait to be all the weight I need to cast most of the time. Once in a while, if the creek that I am fishing is large or swift, I might add a small split shot so my bait nears the bottom where the fish are, as long as it still drifts naturally.

The best place for catching stocked trout is usually very close or right at where the trout were put into the creek when they were planted. When planted trout are stocked into a creek, they usually remain very near that area or will move to a pool or slower spot nearby. I have heard that stocked trout are given a drug to relax them for transport and to keep them from shocking, but I have never verified this. These planter trout like to hang in a school, so when you do catch one, stay in that area until you have fished it thoroughly and then move on. Much of the time, you will have your limit before you move!

When you are fishing for planted trout a few days after they have been planted, you will find they will have separated and scattered throughout the stream. However, they seldom travel very far, and you will catch many more fish if you stay within a hundred yards of the planting area than if you hike the stream a long distance as you would when fishing for wild trout. If you are fishing for planted trout weeks after the first planting, then these more distant places might be good because the trout have become comfortable and are feeding more naturally and have moved away from where all the people and activity are. If the trout have been fished out from the most recent planting, hiking upstream or downstream might be your best bet for a great, relaxing experience whether you catch many or not.

The best lures for catching planted trout are the same as catching wild trout. I use a Panther Martin lure only. I use only the black with yellow dots and gold spinner or the black with red dots and gold spinner. Some folks prefer a Kastmaster or Mepps, but trust me on this, use what I recommend!

If you are fishing for stocked trout with kids or folks who don't get around too good, find a slower, deeper hole in the creek that is easily accessible and close to where the trout were planted in the creek. Put a heavier split shot or two on and cast it out, then let it sit like you would if you were catfishing. This is a great way for anyone to catch planted trout because they are concentrated in these deep pools. I have limited out many times fishing this way when they weren't biting anywhere else! It's great when you can trout fish in a stream while sitting in a lawn chair drinking a beer! Another great benefit of catching planted trout is that they feed all day, and even better, later after the sun is on the water rather than first thing in the morning, like wild trout. They are accustomed to being fed at the hatchery when the workers get there, so there is no need to get up at the butt crack of dawn to have a good trout fishing trip!

Best lures for stream fishing and how to fish with them

Panther Martin lures

In my opinion, Panther Martin lures are by far the best lures for catching trout in streams. Using a lure when fishing for trout in a stream requires that it look like something trout naturally feed on, that it can be casted with accuracy, and that the retrieve can begin before the lure hits the bottom and picks up moss or snags. I have used a lot of lures for catching trout in streams over the years, and I have long ago come to the conclusion that Panther Martin lures are the best lures for trout fishing in creeks. Matter of fact, when I go stream fishing for German brown trout, brook trout, or even rainbow trout, I leave with four or five Panther Martin lures as my entire tackle box! The only lure I use when trout fishing

I know some of you will have a different opinion because you have always used rooster tails, cast masters, or some other favorite lure that you were introduced to. However, you better grab some Panthers and head to your favorite trout-fishing stream and try them out before you argue too adamantly. You can try different colors, but the only ones that I use are the black body ones with the yellow dots and gold spinner, or the black body with the red dots and gold spinner. Occasionally, I will use the all-black with the black spinner, but that is a rare occasion because I am usually limited out before I can change lures.

The best-sized lure for fishing in streams is usually the eighth-ounce one. There is often a breeze in the mountains following the creek through the canyon or meadow, and the sixteenth-ounce one is simply too light to cast any distance with accuracy. Any bigger, and the lure has a tendency to sink too fast and pick up moss as well as be less attractive to the fish. When fishing rainbow trout with lures, you have to keep in mind that their mouths are much smaller than German brown and brook trout. Rainbows feed primarily on bugs in the creeks, but I have cut full-sized mice from the gut of big browns or brook trout! Nowadays, I only keep small trout and release all the larger ones as well as most of the small ones to preserve the population. I will often remove the three-pronged hook from the Panther Martin and replace it with a single hook with the barb pressed in with pliers so as to make it barbless. I miss a few, but who cares!

Fishing small creeks in meadows is one of my favorite types of trout fishing. This is where you are more apt to find those big German browns and brook trout. Many times the stream is only four or five feet wide in some places with undercut grassy banks, willow trees, and brush hanging in the water, and with small ponds every now and then caused by beaver dams. There are often fallen logs laying in the creek or traversing it. The water speed varies, as does the depth of the water, and all these factors make for some interesting and challenging fishing. Unlike planted trout, the trout that I like to pursue are very wild and wary. Casting with accuracy is essential because you may be trying to land your lure fifty or sixty feet away in a three-foot wide creek with a bush hanging over it half the distance you are casting. This can be tricky when you are fishing with four-pound test, a eighth-ounce lure, and the wind is blowing sideways! When fishing lures in small streams, I like to cast upstream. I seem to be much more successful with this than casting downstream. This also adds a complicated dimension to the fishing experience because if the current is flowing at you, you have a little loop in the line from the wind, and if the creek is shallow and mossy on the bottom few inches, you better be on your game! But that is the exact reason I enjoy this fishing so much. If your cast hangs up in the moss, trees, or grass, you have just ruined that stretch of the creek for fishing because when you have to walk up to get untangled or cause a commotion in the water, the wild trout will hide and not bite. This is why it is always prudent to fish close-in first and then cast further distances in subsequent casts. That way, if you do have to disturb the creek, you have already fished it or will be ruining a smaller portion of it as you address the snag or problem.

The best time to fish with lures for trout in streams is either at the very first light of the day or at the last light of the evening. I personally like fishing in meadows for trout at the end of the day. The winds seem to calm, the air is quiet, and the fish are "ringing" in the waters ahead. The big browns and brook trout only feed at this time of the day, although you can catch the smaller ones midday if you don't mind screwing up that stream for fishing at prime time!

Fishing for trout with lures in large streams is a little different, but it too is best done at the same times of day. Those have faster-moving water and deeper pools and are much more forgiving on the casting. In the swifter water, I usually cast downstream or across the creek because snagging is such a problem. I will carefully select my particular eddy or riffle or other fishing spot (see my article about "the drift") and guide the lure strategically into it. In the pools, I will often cast upstream where the riffle falls into the pool and reel downstream because this is where the trout await the next meal. Being sneaky is still important if you are fishing wild trout but nowhere near as critical as fishing in meadows and in small streams. These Panthers are also great for planted trout as well. Give them a try. I guarantee that you might catch a fish!

A sure-fire method for fishing from shore in lakes with Power Bait

Catching trout with power bait in lakes is usually the most effective way of fishing from shore, especially if the fish are stocked there. Using power bait to catch trout when fishing in lakes requires a simple, but essential, power bait setup that allows the power bait to float off the bottom of the lake eighteen inches or so, where the fish are feeding and can see it. Power bait naturally floats, so it is just a matter of baiting it correctly.

I like to use the multi colored "rainbow" power bait, but some folks like the lime green or other colors. Regardless of the color, most will agree that using the power bait with the sparkles in it is always best. This is true when fishing with power bait in streams for planted trout as well. Baiting power bait on a hook is done using a small three-pronged hook. You can use a single hook, but our best success has always been with a three-pronged hook. The power bait is rolled into little round balls about the size of one and a half or two peanuts or so, and the small treble hook is pushed down into this ball of power bait and squeezed on firmly to hide the hook.

Rigging for using power in lakes for trout is simple. Just slide a small egg sinker onto the line through the hole in the center and tie a swivel on to the end of the line to hold the egg sinker on. Make sure the swivel is just large enough so it doesn't get caught in the hole in the egg sinker and get pinched in it. This gives you a sliding sinker setup. Tie on about eighteen inches of leader line, then the three-pronged hook, and you are done. When fishing in lakes with power bait in this fashion, you may have to adjust the amount of leader that you are using because of a number of factors. For instance, if there is heavy growth of weeds on the bottom that sticks up eighteen inches, you may want to extend your leader so your power bait floats above those weeds. Or, the fish might be hanging out at a higher location for some reason.

When fishing for trout with power bait in lakes, you will have to find the area of the lake that the fish are schooled up in. By that, I mean a couple of things. One is that the fish just seem to like certain areas of the shoreline better than others, most likely due to the slope of the bank out into the water and the type of bottom it has, such as small pebbles or sand. We seem to have our best power baitfishing in areas with smaller rocks and a gentle slope, where it is shallow for a long way out, but sloping. Secondly, from day to day the fish seem to gather either closer in or further out from the shore, so we will cast out as far as we can, then a little closer, and then right near the bank until we find them. Once we do, the fishing usually gets hot. If they are in close, a lot of times we will fish using a Panther Martin lure, particularly the black with yellow spots and gold spinner, or the black with red spots and gold spinner. Oddly enough, sometimes they won't touch the lure and other times you catch one every cast. In any case, even if they aren't biting the lure, they will always bite the power bait. If you go to a lake and a particular color is working good, that same color will probably be good year after year.

A secret technique for trolling near shore for lake trout

Trolling for lake trout in the spring near the shore is one of the best lake trout fishing techniques that I know. Knowing how to troll for trout in lakes along with how to rig for trolling in lakes without downriggers are important tips, and one of the trout-trolling techniques that I will share with you here will be different from what you expect, but it's the best technique for lake fishing that I have found. It involves trolling in shallow water very near the shore with very little weight. Fishing in this way, the fish hit hard and the fight is outstanding!

The best time to catch lake trout when trolling is early in the morning before the boat traffic has scared them from the shallows. If there is no boat traffic, the fishing can be good all day. Limits of big lake trout can be common using this relatively unheard of method.

The best bait for trolling for lake trout is either minnows or night crawlers. Using minnows for catching lake trout is my first choice of bait, and I use the largest minnows that I can get (three or four inches). I use about a number six hook and hook it from inside of the mouth, upwards through the "nostril" area. When baiting a minnow for trolling, don't "sew" the minnow's mouth shut with the hook and it will stay alive longer. I tie the hook to the line and leave about eight inches of line dangling so I can tie on a trailer hook about four inches back so it is near the end of the minnow's tail. This trailer hook isn't hooked to anything and is kept behind the baitfish by the movement through the water when trolling. You will increase your success at catching lake trout by over a hundred percent using a trailer hook when trolling. I use a small three-pronged hook for the trailer hook, but you can use a regular hook if that is all you have. I use the same trolling rig for fishing with night crawlers also. When trolling with night crawlers, thread the night crawler onto the hook and up the line with a worm threader so the hook is a third of the way down the worm. Again, use the trailer hook in the same manner. In either case, use one large split shot about eighteen inches ahead of the bait for weight or three small ones and adjust if needed.

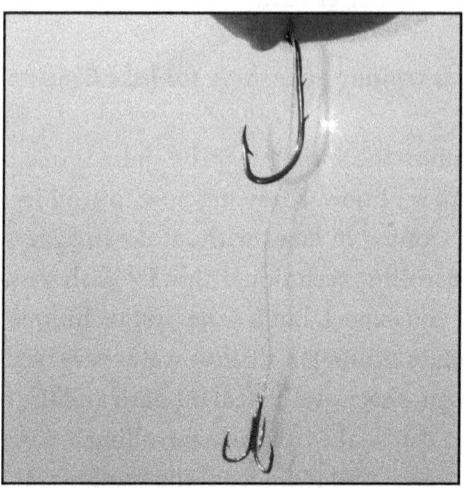

Typical trailer hook set-up

Troll for lake trout using this method during the late winter and early spring. Troll right next to the shore on somewhat steep-sloped areas, which are very common in reservoirs. You will be trolling so that the edge of the boat is often between six and ten feet from shore. The water is clear and shallow, and you would think that by driving the boat in six feet of water with a gas motor that every trout would scatter, but this is not the case. You will be trolling at a pretty good pace (trout swim fast) with your line out behind the boat just thirty yards or so, and those big lake trout will about yank the pole out of the boat! You will be trolling along the shore, which will be meandering along. As you turn the boat on an inward curve, you will have to edge the boat out a little deeper to keep your line from snagging and coming too close to shore. When turning outward towards the far bank, you will have to speed up the boat to make the lure rise so as not to get snagged. It may sound complicated, but if you watch your line when trolling, it comes natural.

Sometimes you can add a little weight and troll further from the shore and find the fish a little deeper if they aren't biting nearer in. You can also try a Castmaster lure or a Panther Martin for trolling as well. Don't be afraid to experiment if they aren't biting, and always keep your eye out for other fishermen who seem to be successful. The best lake trolling techniques can always be found by spying on the two local old farts in the rickety old aluminum boat!

When you catch lake trout by trolling this way, your tackle for trolling is just the hook and a little split shot. It is just you and the fish, and this will make for one of the best trout fishing trips you will ever have. Some folks fish with a string of flashers and a lot of weight, and it kills the fishing experience. Downriggers give you this same experience, but I seldom use one because after spring I am after other fish.

BLACK BASS FISHING
(Largemouth, smallmouth, others)

Author's buddy with a lunker bass

Sight fishing for bass in the spring on their nests

Sight fishing largemouth bass is a favorite type of bass fishing for many black bass fishermen. Fishing for bass while they are on their nests is one of the most popular bass fishing techniques employed by bass fishermen during the springtime. The bass spawn in shallow water when the water temperature reaches the mid sixty-degree range, and they are often visible from the surface on their nests. These males, who build and guard the nest, are very aggressive and will attack any invader with full force and the intent to kill. Seeing the bass on their nests as you search along for them, and then casting into their nesting area, is called sight fishing for black bass. Catching bass while they are spawning by teasing these future fathers with a "creature" bait, such as a frog, lizard, fish, or other lifelike lure, can be a highly productive bass fishing method and one of the most exciting bass fishing methods you can find.

These largemouth bass, spotted bass, smallmouth bass, and other black bass move up into coves and weed beds in shallow water in the spring when the water temperature reaches about sixty-five degrees, depending on the species. I have a chart at the end of the book on the temperatures at which these bass spawn, as well as for muskie, pike, catfish, and many other game fish. Bass like water about three or four feet deep for spawning, but this is not a hard and fast fact. For instance, in delta areas where the water is tidal, the bass might nest in four or five feet of water when the tide is out, which may be five feet deeper when the tide is in. Also, you may find bass nests laid on the stabilizer plates on the back of boats in harbors that haven't been moved for some time, which are only a foot or eighteen inches deep. Matter of fact, you might find largemouth bass nests on both stabilizers, which are five feet apart, that two females laid that are fathered by, and guarded by, the same male. You will see the male bass's fins sticking out of the water while he swims between them, attacking the perch, crappie, crawfish, other bass, and everything else that comes near.

The female bass, which are the bigger bass, are there long enough to lay their eggs and then leave. You may see them in shallow water, but they are not inclined to bite your bait at all, which can be frustrating. After all, you might be looking at a twelve-pounder swimming right in front of your face and ignoring every bait you tease them with, while that four-pound male is more than eager to strike. Many times in a tournament, you have that winning fish right in front of your face, but you would be much wiser to move along and search for that large aggressive male than to waste your time on a huge female that isn't going to give you the time of day.

When sight fishing in shallow water, you can't just motor your boat up on the fish with reckless abandon. They are there to guard the nest but they aren't stupid. You need to spot them from a distance of forty or fifty feet and accurately cast from there. Using polarized glasses for sight fishing is important for spotting bass on their nests. It cuts down the glare and reflection so you can see more clearly below the water. When you see the bass on its nest, you will cast your creature bait, weighted to sink with a "drop shot" rig or some other way, beyond the bass nest so as not to spook him, and you will then drag it into the nesting area and begin to tease the fish. You will have the bait baited so the hook is at the "head" of the bait you are using, as the spawning male bass will attack the head of the predator in order to kill it because he knows biting it in the tail is futile. If you are fishing in weed beds, you will be rigging your rubber worm, lizard, frog, crawfish, or whatever is your bait of choice. The murkier the water, the larger line you can use, but if you are fishing in clear water in a lake, you will want to use fine line so the fish doesn't see it. You might use thirty-pound test braided line in murky water in the delta and a big one-aught hook, but in a clear lake, you might use eight-pound test and a sharp, thin hook. You need a thinner hook with lighter line so when you set the hook, it goes in without too much resistance because the line will stretch. Yanking a large hook in with thirty-pound test is no problem, but that large hook isn't going to set well when that hook hits a bone or cartilage and the line stretches a foot over the fifty feet it is out. Always make sure you use good-quality, sharp hooks for sight fishing largemouth bass and other fish.

When you are motoring along the shore looking for bass on their nests, move slowly and keep your distance. Many fishermen stop using the trolling motor and propel themselves with a pole to be more stealthy and quiet. Avoid making unnecessary noise or rapid movements. And when possible, release the bass where you caught it. It will dart right back to its nest in minutes.

Black bass spawn usually two or three or even more times per year, so the spring sight fishing season can be quite long, albeit best in the early season when the water temperature for bass spawning is just right. Also, water temperatures vary from place to place, so the season is somewhat different in each and sometimes even in different areas of the same lake, river, or pond. Additionally, the spawning temperature for smallmouth, spotted bass, and other strains are different, which can vary your fishing habits. Having a boat is great for sight fishing, but they are usually spawning near shore and can be gotten easily by casting down the shoreline. Check out the chart at the end of this book for the different bass spawning temperatures, and make sure you don't miss this exciting fishing opportunity!

A couple of the most-effective methods for using Senko worms

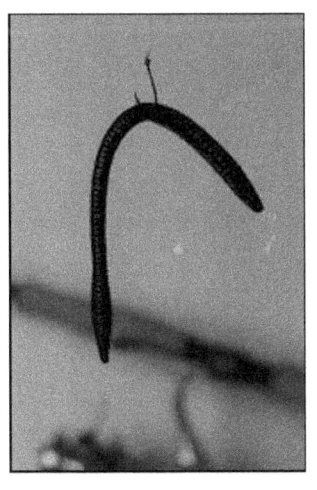

Wacky worm set-up

Knowing how to use Senko worms for bass fishing is a must for all bass fishermen. Fishing with Senkos is a great way of catching post-spawn bass in the spring, and using Senko worms when the fish are in deeper water at any time is always worth a try when you are having trouble catching them. Rigging the Senko can be done either in a weedless Texas style or by rigging it in a "wacky" manner, or less commonly with some weight.

Senko rubber worms are very plain-looking giant grub worm type fishing lures. Senko worms look like a fat worm shaped about like your pinkie finger, about as big around as your finger, with both ends bluntly shaped about the same as the end of your finger. I like the big ones that are thick and six or more inches long. They come in different colors, but I like the darker brown-looking ones with the watermelon-red, big sparkles in them or the one that is brown with a night crawler looking color on bottom. Senko worms are heavy, as far as rubber worms go. They sink readily without weight and remain horizontal, for the most part, as they do. Like any sinking lure or bait, many of your strikes happen during this descent, so you have to watch your line as it sinks for that hit. Senkos are permeated and saturated in salt through and through. Most freshwater lakes and reservoirs are nearly absent of salt in an amount sufficient enough to satisfy the needs of the bass living there, and most of them are constantly craving salt. This, in my opinion, is one of the major reasons why fishing with Senko worms is such a good fishing method. The fish smell this salty treat and cannot resist it.

One of the best Senko fishing methods is to simply cast the Senko, let it sink to the bottom and sit, and simply "baitfish" with it. I know this may sound odd, but it is a great way to catch bass. You just shove your big 1-0 to 3-0 hook through the head and hook it back through so the tip of the hook is in the cut-out groove made to house it so it is exposed out of the rubber but still weedless. Casting a Senko usually needs no weight, as the worm itself is so heavy. It is best to keep your distance from your fishing area and cast into it from afar so you don't make the fish wary. Some people will cast a Senko with an underhand toss thirty feet from their target, whereas I like to zing it out there sixty or more feet, or as far as I can cast it.

Fishing Senko worms in grass beds that are three to ten feet deep is also an effective Senko fishing method. Out from the old nesting areas where the water is a little deeper and maybe near a drop-off is another place to try. Just move slow and let it sink and sit. Keep a little loop in your line so as not to move the Senko but still see a hit. Much of the time the hit is subtle because the bass come and "inhale" the Senko instead of strike it, so you may see only a tightening of the loop in the line or feel subtle resistance when you lift your pole tip from time to time. You can experiment with depth on each fishing trip until you find them.

Casting into deeper water with the hook "wacky rigged" is a very popular and productive Senko fishing technique. Simply jam the hook one time through the middle of the Senko so it hangs down on both sides. Then cast it and let it sink while you stand on guard for that hit on the way down. You can also let it sit a while on the bottom this way, too. Don't be afraid to jig the Senko with little twitches when it is falling or sitting on the bottom to tease the fish a little if there is no action. A little change might be the trick.

One friend of mine rigs the Senko weedless with some split shot about eighteen inches in front of it and uses a small swivel just below the split shot to keep the line from twisting up. Then he casts out and retrieves the Senko ever so slowly, with some twitches as well as letting it sèt occasionally. The bass must think the Senko is some sort of eel or something slithering on the bottom. Regardless, when they get close enough to sense that salt, they can't resist hitting it. Make sure that you keep a couple of Senkos in your tackle box when you head out bass fishing because they just might be the trick!

Simple advice and tips for using crankbaits

When fishing with a crankbait for bass, you must consider a few key factors. These factors are primarily what is the best color crankbait for the area you are fishing, what is the best depth to fish crankbaits, and how to fish with a crankbait for best results. As you will come to see, only actually trying different types of crankbaits and fishing them at different depths and around different structures will actually answer these crankbait fishing questions for certain. However, there are a few tips that are helpful to begin with, and I will share a few of my thoughts with you here, including my favorite colors of crankbaits and how I like to fish them, along with where to use a deep-diving crankbait, where to use a shallow-diving crankbait, as well as using the mid-diving crankbait.

Let's be clear that I am not a pro bass fisherman of any sort, and I will typically own a very limited tackle selection that is both uncomplicated and simple. It will consist of less than a dozen of the best crankbaits I have found (some deep divers, mediums, and shallows), a half dozen spinnerbaits, and a few Senko worms. My tackle selection is adequate for most bass fishing trips without being exorbitant in cost or overly confusing. I personally think that the best colors of crankbaits are crawdad-colored, chartreuse, silver, and blue, or like a shad or bluegill or some combination of these. But one time my buddy and I did a float trip for nine days down the upper Sacramento River (ah, the good ol' college days!), and we bought some long minnow-looking crankbaits out of the "dollar box" that were fluorescent orange on the bottom with a bill on the front that was short and mounted sideways so the bait swam on its side. We had the hugest success with those, more than I have ever had with a crankbait. We caught smallmouth, largemouth, squawfish, and even a channel cat on those damn things and never found them in any bait shop again! Best dollar investment I ever made. I usually start with the crawfish or chartreuse/silver or a bluegill type in shallow water and use the more blues and silvers in the deeper waters at first, but switch it up if they aren't working. Crawdads like to hang out in rocks in rivers in the deep areas, so that may be the lure of choice. You'll know when you start catching fish!

As far as what kind of crankbait is best when it comes to their diving depth, it depends on where you are fishing and when. Personally, I find myself fishing with a shallow diving crankbait seventy-percent of the time. I am often fishing in the spring in shallow water or "sight fishing" bass on their nests, and there is usually grass, sticks, or some sort of cover on the bottom, so the shallow-diving crankbait works for me. Later in the year, I might be fishing out in the main river or in deeper areas of a lake where there are some deeper trees that have fallen in from the bank, or I am fishing the outer edge of some grass or weeds where the water is deeper, and I like to drag a medium-depth crankbait over the branches. At times, we will fish points in manmade lakes where the banks are steep or around riprapped banks in the river and use the deep divers, but for me this isn't often because by this time my spear-fishing and abalone-diving habits have kicked in and my weekends are taken! Deep divers are great in summer for finding and fishing the bass when they are schooled up and the water is warm on top.

One thing I have learned about fishing a crankbait is that the fish seem to always like some irregular event that causes the lure to act "jerky." For instance, dragging it over branches or using the pole tip to jerk it around a little is much better than a straight retrieve. Don't be hesitant to try the straight retrieve, as that may be what the big bass are in the mood for that day, but mix it up. It might even be that white spinner bait they are waiting for instead of a crankbait, so mix it up to find the fish!

The longer and straighter "lips" on the front of a spinnerbait indicate one that is deeper diving, and the shorter-lipped ones are the shallower-diving ones and so on. One thing to know is that the heavier the line you use, or I should say bulkier, the less depth you get out of any crankbait. This isn't so important, if at all, in shallow crankbait fishing, but it can be the difference between getting to the fish or not when fishing deep-diving crankbaits. It is just something to keep in mind. Also, speaking of fishing with deep-diving crankbaits, they are at their deepest at the end of the retrieve just before you start reeling them to the boat, so choosing your fishing position on the water is important to reach your desired target spot. Using lighter line to get that longer cast and a longer period in that deep "sweet spot" as you retrieve the lure might be the ticket for deep fishing, so keep this in mind.

Many fishermen swear that to have the best crankbait fishing success, the lure has to "run true" or be "tuned." Basically, what they are talking about is simply turning the "eye" that the line is tied to on the front of the lure one way or the other to make the lure retrieve back in a straight line when reeled. You can pull your lures through the water with your pole or reel close in and watch to see if you need to adjust the eye. Turning it right makes it go more to the left and vice-versa, and it takes a very little amount of turn to change it, so be careful not to get carried away. Many do this after catching each fish and check for this often. I don't bother because after that experience with that orange dollar crankbait that I told you about, I don't find it that important. I have noticed that no matter how it is tuned, the beer in the ice chest seems to disappear at the same rate!

So, the moral of the story is to always carry and try crankbaits because they are essential bass fishing tackle, carry a few of the best-colored crankbaits, carry a couple of colors of different diving depth crankbaits, and try them in different areas and depths where you are fishing.

Spinnerbaits – don't leave home without them

Typical spinner baits

Using spinnerbaits is a great way to catch bass almost anywhere and at any time. Fishing with spinnerbaits is exciting and much easier than you think. Spinnerbait fishing is a method that is easily employed by pro bass fishermen as well as beginners. Fishing with a spinnerbait is not a science, and you will find that just taking a couple of colors with you and actually getting them in the water will lead to catching many nice bass with no need in getting too carried away with technique. And you can certainly trust my opinion because I am a professional weekend warrior!

The best color spinnerbait to use is the one you have in your tackle box because it is a good lure; not using one because you have heard that other colors are better is not a good decision. Hungry bass or a bass ready to kill anything in sight for being too close to its nest are not half as picky as you might think. I always like to keep a white spinnerbait, a chartreuse spinnerbait, and then a darker color or two. I do like a little red on them, but if not, so be it. I rarely add a worm or tail to the spinnerbait, but many do. I can see how it might attract some larger fish and deter the smaller ones.

As far as spinners go, I usually use a single spinner because it is more successful on a consistent basis and they are cheaper. Speaking of cost, I am not big on spending a fortune on tackle. The best spinner baits have ball bearings in the swivels and some other features, but this is not important to me because I know that where I fish the spinnerbait and how it is retrieved are a hundred times more important than some minute detail like this will ever be.

The best color for the spinner on a spinnerbait is silver. Some folks use gold, and I am sure that in some waters that this is a good choice, but I have consistently had the best luck with the silver spinner. I rarely even have a gold spinner in my tackle box, to be honest with you.

Spinnerbaits are made to fish around logs, grass, docks, brush, and such structures. With the hook riding behind the spreader wire and facing upward, you can retrieve it through about anything without getting a snag as you would with a crankbait. I like to use heavy line most of the time (ten to twelve pound), so I can pull it through and around structures without losing it, as well as horse the fish over and under logs and brush.

Retrieving a spinnerbait once you cast is a subject that there are many opinions on. The best way to retrieve a spinnerbait is the way that catches fish, and you can philosophize all you want, but until you get out there and fish, you will not know what is best that day. I start out by retrieving the spinnerbait just under the water, so at times it throws a small wake. Then, I will let it fall a little and retrieve it a little slower so there is no wake and I am fishing a foot or two deep. Sometimes I will shift my rod tip up and down or from side to side to give the spinnerbait a little odd action, like a drunken fish stumbling home from the bar. Other times, I will let it sink deep and reel very slow and drag it over some deeper branches and structures. I usually will try all these in one area before I move on. I like to cast as near the bank as possible and fish out to the boat because who knows where those wily little buggers are hanging out. If I do see one on a nest, I cast as far beyond it as I can and guide it right in to the awaiting bass. If I am fishing from the shore with spinnerbaits, I cast along the bank and hold my pole out beyond the grasses and moss and retrieve it as well as cast over and around any structure I can reach that is further out. The moral of the story is that there is no wrong way to retrieve a spinnerbait, you should try anything that floats your boat at the time, and always have three or four various colored ones in your tackle box.

Fishing small farm ponds

Catching bass in a small farm pond is much different than catching bass in large ponds or lakes. Bass fishing in small ponds requires just a few fishing techniques and tips that I will discuss in this bass fishing article.

Small farm pond fishing differs from fishing large ponds in that the shade and fish habitat are very limited, as is the shape of the bottom. Many times these small farm ponds are simple ovals that are shallow at the shores and evenly and gently sloped to the middle, except for a dam on one end that might drop off deeper more rapidly. These small ponds are usually best fished from the shore and can easily be walked entirely around in a half hour and fished around in an hour or so. There are usually weeds and moss along the shore and often just a tree or two because any trees that do sprout are eaten by the livestock that water there, which is why these ponds were usually built in the first place. Often, the only shade is under these weeds along the banks. Given there are usually few trees, there are few tree stumps or brush for cover. These ponds are often much cooler in the deepest parts in the center or along the dam.

The best time to fish small farm ponds is early in the morning at daybreak or late in the evening. Often, getting there first thing in the morning, rather than in the evening, is best because no one has fished it yet that day. When fishing for bass in a small pond, it is best that the pond hasn't been fished for a few days and not the same day for sure. When fishing for bass in a small pond, you usually will catch ninety-nine percent of the nice bass on the first walk around the pond, and after that, they are spooked for the day or longer. This means fishing in a small farm pond is best done alone, and if you do fish with someone, either move slowly and take turns or fish in different directions and accept that you will each get to fish half of the pond. You might even agree to a place in the pond where you will each fish to so that it is evenly split and there is no racing each other! Flip a coin for who gets which direction if one is better.

I like to use a spinnerbait to catch bass in a small pond if the weeds aren't too thick. If there is a lot of grass, weeds, or moss in the water, I like to use a weedless frog or other weedless top water plug. You can also rig a weedless worm and work it like a snake across the weeds as well, but whatever you cast must have some weight to it for casting a long distance. These bass in these shallow farm ponds are right on the shore, and if they see you and you spook them, they are gone for good. Nothing is worse than seeing the swirl of a ten pounder as it darts away for cover. This is when you need a boot behind you that you can pull a string on and kick yourself in the butt for blowing it! Move slowly and quietly, taking a few steps at a time and casting ahead a good distance so you don't scare your prey! Also, remember that when you do catch a bass in a farm pond, that all the bass that you drag the one on your line through will dart away, and your fishing for them is done for the day. Fish the pond in small increments so you don't ruin your own fishing. Cast fifty feet or so, walk ten feet, and then cast fifty feet again so you are only fishing ten feet of the pond at a time. That way, if you do hook up, you haven't ruined the area ahead of that point.

Later in the day, when the water heats up, you might find the bass laying in the deep part of the pond by using a rubber worm or Senko worm if you are lucky. Make sure you bring some night crawlers, too, and a bobber because the bluegill are usually thick and that is some fun fishing and great eating. And you can fish these all day after the bass fishing is done.

Remember that when you are fishing in small farm ponds for bass that it is a small pond and you can fish all the big bass out in no time and wreck the fishing for yourself and others. Release the big bass for fun later, and don't hesitate to take a few small ones for the table to put with the perch!

CATFISH, CRAPPIE, PERCH, BLUEGILL, AND PAN FISH

Panfish, my favorite eating fish!

Catching perch, bluegill, rock bass, and other pan fish – The "meeting them halfway" technique

Some of the most fun fish to catch are the perch, bluegill, sunfish, and pan fish, including the red ear and the rock bass, and they have the benefit of being some of the best-tasting fish you can eat. Learning how to employ these simple tricks will truly enhance your fun and bragging rights, and teaching a kid this method will most certainly cause them to be hooked on fishing for their lifetime.

Catching them is trickier than what meets the eye. Sure, you can throw on a piece of night crawler with a bobber and let it sit and you will eventually catch something, but you can increase your catch enormously with a little technique.

First, I like to fish for pan fish when the sun is on the water, but where there is a little shade from trees and tules. I personally think that these fish, which easily fit right into a largemouth bass's mouth, are more apt to be active and feeding when they are less worried about ending up there, which certainly is more likely when the bass bite is active, such as in the mornings and evenings. But still, these little perch like to hang pretty near some structure to hide in if that hungry black bass decides for a midday snack.

Using the right-sized hook is important, as is the right-sized split shot fishing weight. The hook should be big enough to hold that chunk of night crawler (about a third of one), threaded up over the fishhook's eye with the hook protruding at the bottom so that the worm is straight, as opposed to having a "U" shape like the hook has. Threading the fishing worm rather than sewing it on so that it is bunched up on the hook also seems to have the effect of making the bait last much longer, along with causing the fish to bite better. Many fishermen use much too small of a hook. The hook should be about a number six. Rock bass, which are found in schools in certain waters, can take a little larger hook because they have a slightly larger mouth.

The weight (split shot) should be as small as possible to allow the worm to sink and the bobber to be held upright. The bobber should be small and the fishing line lightweight—I like four-pound test. Basically, this rig is set up to allow a minimum of interference with you and your fishing pole, and the hook itself when you are toying with the bluegill or other pan fish of your prey. Too big of a bobber requires too much weight to upright. I like the good old red and white bobber, but my dad likes the pencil type bobber because it is a little more delicate and streamlined to allow even less resistance in the fishing technique that I will explain here.

Trust me on this— those sunfish, perch, and bluegill are wily little buggers. They test their prey, in most cases, before they consume it. They come up and grab the worm with their lips and nibble and tug on it before they gulp it down. If they feel any resistance on this test, they spit it out. They will come right back to it, or another one in the school will, but again they will toy with it and test it for their safety. It is funny how fish seem to have a sense that us humans are after them and keep their guards up at all times! Perch are especially wary. This is where the technique is important, and where the use of the proper tackle that we talked about above comes into play.

To catch these sly little fish, the trick is what I call "meeting them halfway." They will grab the hook lightly and begin to swim away from the school. At this point, you will easily lift the line from the water to the bobber without moving the bobber, and let the fish cause the line to tighten to your fishing rod tip. At that point, a very small flick of the wrist to set the hook is in order, not a full yank, as just the tightening of the line to a taunt line is usually enough of a hook set, but a little flick at that key moment is best. It is important that you not have slack line lying too far across the water between your rod tip and the bobber, as to take up this slack during a bite will certainly move the bobber, and the fish will feel the resistance and release the bait. A heavy bobber is built-in resistance that the fish don't like, as is heavy line or too much weight. The key is not letting the fish sense any resistance until that moment when they experience the wrist-snapping hook set. Most of the time, they will feel you on the other end of the line and release the bait until the one time when the feel to both you and them is such that no movement is sensed and the line tightens between you and the fish – hence the term "meeting them halfway."

Some will argue that it is much easier to catch these fish than this how-to lesson portrays, and when the fish are full of roe and eating for a thousand that is somewhat true. But when the fish are living their day-to-day lives the rest of the year, you will find this fishing technique essential to fill that stringer for the big fish fry. Even when they are about to spawn, this fishing tip will undoubtedly lead to you being the king of the pan fish anglers!

Knowing how to cook and eat these delicate freshwater fish is a must or it can be frustrating. First, you simply scale the fish (I like using a butter knife), cut their heads off, gut, and rinse them. I never use a batter because it is too fattening and overwhelms the flavor of any seafood. I simply wet the fish with water and bread them in a mixture of one part flour, one part cornmeal, and one part seasoned breadcrumbs with a generous amount of garlic powder (not garlic salt) and salt and pepper to taste. Then I fry them in a deep pool of high heat oil like peanut oil or canola oil until they are golden brown. A deep fryer works best. You will find that the cornmeal has a magic quality in it to keep the fish from burning too brown and allows a little forgiveness for overcooking. The cooking is quick and active, much like the fishing for these fish.

When they are done, just remember that there is a bone in the center with a nice little fillet on each side. Pull the fins out of the top and bottom with your hands (they will come out easily) and clean any fine bones left there. Then, slice your fork from the tail forward with it flat against the center bone and the fillet for that side will come right off. Turn it over and scoop the rib bones from the gut area of the fillet and repeat the same for the other side. Squeeze a little lemon and enjoy. I like eating the crispy fins, and the roe sacs of the females are excellent and are prepared the same way. Remember to use a screen to cover the roe if you cook them because they pop worse than you can imagine and can burn you or your spouse's you-know-what when that grease covers the walls! And, by the way, I use that same breading for striped bass, frog legs, abalone, and about every other type of fish and seafood. I will also sometimes prepare a little tartar sauce with mayo, sweet pickle relish, garlic, and lemon juice to dip the fillets in. All this goes best if you leave the forks in the drawer and use your hands to eat it! Bon appétit!

Catching crappie with minnows and jigs

Catching crappie has always been one of my favorite kinds of fishing. Not only is it usually productive and relatively fast action, they are definitely one of my favorite fish to eat. Nothing makes a better picture or story than a five-foot stringer of crappie and the ensuing fish fry that comes with it!

Crappie are a fish that like to hang out near structures such as branches, rocks, and boat docks where they are protected from bigger predator fish and have some shade. Like any fish, they are most hungry and bite the best when they are getting ready to spawn, but they can be caught year round by changing from backwaters to more deep waters and to areas with steeper banks and with some structure, such as pylons, piers, agricultural pump intakes, and such, and fishing them at deeper depths.

Crappie like to eat smaller fish, and minnows are the best bait to use to catch them. This is usually done with a bobber, one small split shot weight put on the line about fifteen inches above the hook, which is on the end of the fishing line. When baiting the minnow on the hook, just hook the minnow through the back under the dorsal fin. The hook is about a number six or smaller if the fish you are catching are small. When you buy minnows, they come in a couple of sizes, and you will want the small ones. If I am going crappie fishing, I never leave without two or three dozen in my minnow bucket and five or six dozen if the fishing is hot! Make sure you use a minnow bucket and get it into the lake or water where you are fishing as soon as you can because they will start dying. If you will not have them in the water for an hour or more, stop anywhere and squirt fresh water in the bucket with a hose so it aerates the water.

I like to use minnows for fishing from the shore in ponds, lakes, sloughs, and such, but if I am fishing off a dock or where I can jig with a crappie lure, that is my preferred way to catch crappie. When they hit the jig and you hook them, they take off hard and it is exciting. You seldom have more than three to six feet of line out, so the action is quick when you do get one. Often you just lift them out with your pole and there is no reeling involved. I like to use an ultra-light pole with a four-pound test line whether I am bobber fishing with minnows or using a crappie jig. Mini-twisters are the most popular crappie jig these days, but I have always liked the little white feathery jig with the big silver bug-eyes. It has been around a long time and still works, which is funny because they seem to have stopped working on shad for some reason. I like to use white for the tail sections and usually red for the head sections of my jig, although white and chartreuse or all white are popular too.

Typical crappie jigs

The line is tied directly to the eye of the jig, and the weight of the jig is usually all you need. You will walk (or float in a boat) along the dock, pier, or other structure and raise and lower the jig in an area about two or three feet in distance while flipping it with your wrist to give it a fishy type action as though it were swimming or even wounded. You move around the structure, changing depths of the area that you are fishing in quite often until you find the school, which crappie are almost always found in when spawning. Then, you note that depth and stick with it and the area until the bite stops, and then off you go to repeat the process again. During the spawning season, you will find that the depth of the next school will most likely be similar to where you caught the last ones. Before or after the spawn, they travel in ones and twos so you have to keep on the move around the dock or structure.

I like to fish little sloughs, inlets, harbors, and backwaters, but they are where they are, and friends of mine fish right on the banks of the main channels, especially in midsummer.

Cleaning crappie is easy. Just scrape the scales off with a knife, cut the head off, and pull the innards out with your index finger. Then bread them with a mixture of cornmeal, flour, and seasoned breadcrumbs in equal parts along with a little garlic powder, salt, and pepper and fry them in deep and hot oil. A deep fryer works best. Squeeze some lemon and eat. I wish I was there!

Catching bullhead and yellow catfish

Catching bullhead catfish can be fast and furious fishing when they are about to spawn. The water temperature for bullhead catfish to spawn is between 79 and 89 degrees but much colder when their eggs and sperm are first developing; these yellow catfish bite best during this period. This time, when the water is cold and clear, is the best time for catching yellow catfish because their meat is firm and mild to the taste. Later, when the water warms up, they can get a little mushy and muddy tasting, but they are one of the best-eating catfish if you get them at the right time and place. Catching them is easy and fun. Here is the trick.

Usually, the bullhead catfish bite best in the early summer. These yellow catfish bloat up with eggs and sperm, and they feed aggressively all day and bite even better at night. They are usually in large schools, and when you start catching them, you very often will catch two catfish at a time. These catfish only grow to be an average of about nine or ten inches, but they bite hard, and you have to jerk to set the hook in those hard catfish mouths. It is probably one of the best types of fishing for kids there is, along with perch and bluegill fishing with a bobber, because they are easy to catch. When you get into them, you can catch a hundred or more a day! It will be one of the most memorable fishing trips that your kids or grandkids will ever have. I am almost sixty, and I still remember my friends and I catching a hundred in a night while fishing off the shore of an island in the delta, with our parents there to keep the fish going on the stringer and the bait going on the hook!

Fishing for bullhead catfish is also an inexpensive fishing trip. All that is needed is the pole and reel, some cheap hooks, and some one-ounce weights. The hooks are about sixes or any size that will wrap around the tip of your index finger without poking you but fitting snugly. You fish with two hooks. The hooks are of the type that already have the string on them, with the hook on one end and a loop on the other. They are common at Wal-Mart or any tackle shop. Get the cheapest for this type of fishing because you will lose them, and they are plenty sharp enough for this activity. It is not as if you are going to lose some record bullhead catfish, after all! Don't use a fishing leader, either. Just grab the line where you want the hook so you have a loop and tie it in a knot so the loop remains in the line. Again, think cheap and easy! The bottom hook loop is tied about eighteen inches above the weight, which is just tied directly to the bottom of the line. The second hook loop is up above the first about fourteen inches. Then just slip the loop on the hook over the other loop and run the hook through the line's hoop; pull it tight and you are done. All this virtually with no tackle other than the weight and hooks.

The best bait for catching bullhead catfish in most areas are clams, worms, and crawfish tails if you can get them. The river clams take a little time to open, and you may have to use a couple of them if they are too small to cover the hook. Worms are always a good choice. Some folks swear by red worms and some by night crawlers, but both are good bait. They go crazy for peeled crawdad tails, and they stay on the hook good, but you have to find and catch them, which can be a challenge. Some folks like using liver for catfish bait as well, but that is better for channel cats and other bigger catfish. I prefer clams if I can get them and they are decent sized, or night crawlers if they are not.

Then, you need to find a place to catch them. The best place is to go where you have caught them before. They seem to like particular areas for some reason. By that, I mean that you might move down the slough or river fifty or a hundred yards and increase your success tenfold! It is probably the shape or texture of the bottom or some feature such as a deeper hole. Regardless, I know this to be a hundred percent true, so don't hesitate to move around. Then when you find them, remember the spot for the upcoming years because it will probably remain a hot spot.

Catching channel catfish using lures and bait

Channel cat fishing is different from catching bullheads, blue catfish, and others. Channel cats swim faster, are much more aggressive, and like swift water. Channel catfish will feed on the bottom like other types of catfish do, but will just as often feed midway to the bottom and even on the top of the water like a black bass! I have caught many a channel catfish in midsummer along the banks of the colder main stream of the river and then caught them in the warm backwater sloughs while casting spinner baits and crankbaits for black bass. I have caught them on minnows while I was crappie fishing and with night crawlers when I was bluegill fishing, and I have caught them on every type of bass fishing lure that is made! Catching channel catfish is not to be overlooked; a great freshwater game fishing sport as they fight like hell and can get easily over ten pounds.

When I am fishing for channel catfish in swift, swirling water, which they love, I use a sliding sinker setup with about a three- to four-foot leader and enough weight to hold it in the tail of the swift water. I try to get upstream and above whatever is causing the water's turbulence, so I don't need too much weight to hold it. I use a pretty good-sized hook (one to four or bigger) and a whole night crawler or a big chunk of bait. I will use my striped bass fishing equipment with about twelve- to seventeen-pound fishing line with that same weight leader because channel cats don't seem so picky about seeing the leader like some fish are. When they hit you know it! Channel cats have hard mouths, so when you set the hook, really put the wood to him! Channel cats have one thing in common with other catfish in that even though they will bite during the day, the fishing for them is much better at night.

My brother and I used to fish in the main channel of the Sacramento River during midsummer for large and smallmouth bass. The river where we fished is 150 yards wide and flows pretty good. Along some of the banks where the river has eroded away, the cottonwood and other trees have fallen in the water and there are exposed root balls protruding out into the river providing great structure for fish. We would use spinner baits, crankbaits, and big jigs and rubber worms. Almost every day out, we would land a good channel catfish and untold numbers of squawfish, which are a boney pike-type fish that fight like hell as well, along with some nice largemouth bass, which made for a great day on the water!

SHAD FISHING WITH LIGHTWEIGHT FISHING GEAR —
A Fishing Trip Worth Making Every Year

The author and the biggest shad he has ever caught

How to fish for shad in the river

Catching shad in the late spring with ultra-light fishing equipment has to be one of the most enjoyable fishing experiences out there. Shad are not that big, usually between a pound and a half to five pounds, but they fight like they are three times their size! They catch the current with their wide bodies like a schooner captures the wind, and your drag had better be set right or you will be up for a re-rig. The best thing is that on many days you will catch several per hour, and every one is a challenge. By the end of a good shad-fishing day, your you-know-what is kicked and your arm is tired and cramped. Of course, you can't wait to do it all over again the next day!

Shad typically migrate up the rivers to spawn in May and June. The old-timers say that when the white cottonwood seed tufts are blowing in the wind, it is time to fish for shad. It is best to fish them when the wind is calm because the line is usually four-pound test with just a little spit shot or two for weight, and more than a breeze plays havoc with it and makes the bites hard to see or feel. Also, you usually wade into the river on a gravel bar up to your waist, and the wind can make you pretty cold if you prefer shorts instead of waders as my friends and I do.

The most popular lure for shad is the little rubber "mini-twister" on a small jig head with a red front. Most people prefer the chartreuse color mini-twister tail with sparkles in it, but make sure to take a few other colors as well. Hardly anyone uses it, but some days I have had great luck on the salmon-colored one when the green stopped working. Depending on the flow, you will add a small split shot or two up from the jig a foot or so. You want to weight so your jig is right on

Typical shad jig heads

Common shad jig bodies

the bottom because that is where the fish are. You will want to feel the bottom once in a while in your drifts but not too often. Just try to stay off of it by reeling slowly. My favorite is chartreuse with sparkles

Usually, you will find a gravel bar that jets into the river—hopefully with no snags where you are fishing—and wade out. You cast your line out to about a ten o'clock position upstream and let the lure and line sink a few seconds until it floats about straight out in front of you, at which time you take the slack up in the line and hold your pole tip up a little so you can see its action during the balance of the drift. You will let the line drift until nearly straight down from you, and then reel in and repeat the motion. Again, you have to be near the bottom, so you may end up adding or removing weight to get into the bite.

Sometimes when the shad bite, it feels like your line has caught on the rocks and it pulls steady; other times they bite so light that you just see a little nibble on the tip of your pole. Anything causes me to put the wood to them! Every day it seems the bite is different. You might stand twenty feet away from your buddy one day with identical rigging and you will catch ten and he will catch one, and then the next day you are the one on the hind teat. That gets frustrating, let me tell you!

We usually release the shad, but now and then my buddy likes to smoke them, which tastes great. They are pretty oily fish like the sardines that they are related to, and quite bony as well. My mom always liked to cook the roe. She would par-boil it then bread and fry it, which you should certainly try if you have never had it. My mother would also pressure-cook the whole fish to dissolve most of the bones, and then remove the meat with a spoon to get rid of the rest. Then she would mix the meat with garlic, parsley, chives, salt, and pepper and bread it like regular fish, serving up delicious shad patties. MMMMM! My dad used shad for sturgeon bait and Grandma for her roses.

Anyway, if you have never fished shad, give it a try. It is a blast. A lot of anglers fly fish for shad and they have stellar results. I don't fly fish, but I hope to try it soon after I retire and have the time to find someone willing to risk their life to my casting! You definitely don't want to miss this fishing opportunity.

DIVING AND SPEAR FISHING —
no need for scuba equipment for this fun!

Author with day's spearfishing catch

How to spearfish – the spear gun, the Hunt, the gear, and the spear

Spear fishing has to be one of the most exciting, fun, and under-enjoyed water sports out there. It brings the best of two sporting worlds, hunting and fishing, together into one for the outdoorsman who enjoys both of these outdoor activities.

Spear fishing is primarily a saltwater fishing sport, and for the most part is illegal on inland waters, except for carp, which is mostly speared above water by archery. What is important to note is that the majority of spear fishing is done without the use of scuba equipment by holding your breath and "free diving." This may sound difficult, as if you must have extraordinary lung capacity, but this is not the case. Even a novice that can dive to the bottom of a typical swimming pool can expect to have a killer spear fishing adventure without the use of scuba equipment, although spear fishing with it is much easier. This article focuses on free diving primarily, but many of the principles apply when scuba diving as well.

In many areas off the coasts of the mainland United States, the water is often murky, with visibility of only ten or fifteen feet. In contrast, in Hawaii, Mexico, the Caribbean, and other places where the ocean conditions are clear and calm, visibility might be a hundred feet or more. In this clear water, the fish can see you clearly, and you have to hold your breath much longer to allow the fish to become accustomed to you being part of the landscape of the ocean bottom so they relax and swim within range. In this case, scuba tanks come in handy, but the locals will classify you as a "sissy" if they see you, especially in the Hawaiian Islands. The typical range of a spear gun is only the length of the gun plus the length of the cord that attaches the spear to the gun, which is typically a total of about ten feet. The typical spear fishing shot is much shorter than that when spear fishing for lingcod, Cabazon, China cod, halibut, and other bottom fish, which are caught when stationary, lying on the bottom on the rocks, or in the sand in the case of halibut. Here, you can literally swim up and poke many of these fish if you wanted to just scare them off. Your biggest concern when spearing these close-in fish is to keep the tip of your spear far enough away from the fish so as to allow your gun to propel the spear far enough to gain enough velocity to pack that killing wallop to the fish. Shooting from too close is tempting, especially when you are hovering over a record lingcod or any huge fish, but it is a big mistake. Relax and keep your spear tip at least twenty inches from your prey. I like to use a much shorter cord than what usually comes with the spear gun when you purchase it. The spear gun has a catch near the trigger, as well as one up front that the cord is gathered and wrapped around while hunting to keep it from floating around freely and tangling up on you, kelp, your diving buddy, and other things. The rear catch is made so that when you squeeze the trigger, it releases the cord along with the spear. I prefer to shorten the cord from the typical eight to ten or so feet to just five feet. Given most of the fish I shoot are just a couple of feet away, I don't have to worry about wrapping the cord up after every shot and having it tangle on me or other snags while I am hunting fish. The time it takes to re-load my gun is cut in more than half by eliminating this hassle. Furthermore, the cord is a dynamic beast unto itself. You can adjust it all you want to exactly fit the spear gun's cord holders, but that cord's length changes when it is wet, older, or stretched from shooting. The cord's length must be within just a couple of inches or it will not fit snugly between the two catches on the spear gun, and therefore becomes loose and floats free anyway most of the time. My shortened line is made to load the spear gun and let it float freely without it tangling. Unless you are hunting for fish like white bass, tuna, or in clear waters for non-bottom fish that require much longer shots, you will find that this is the only way to go.

I want to mention here that there are typically three types of spear guns. One, the Hawaiian sling, is not really a gun, but a long pole with a large rubber band (surgical rubber) attached at the opposite end of the spearhead. To shoot this spear, this rubber band is inserted in the vee between the thumb and index finger of the same hand that you hold the pole with. You "cock" the spear pole by simply pulling it back to stretch the rubber band, and then grasp the pole until you aim and release the grip to take your shot. Many divers will wrap duct tape several times around the pole shaft where they hold the pole when it is cocked so that it makes a grip that is easier to hold than the bare spear pole, which tends to slip when you are on a long dive chasing a fish and your grip weakens. I prefer to do so.

The Hawaiian sling is a handy fishing tool, and I often prefer to use it over my spear gun. It is great when you are in a big school of blue or black bass that tends to swim in the area halfway from the ocean bottom to the surface, which is usually about six to twenty feet. It allows you to shoot the bass, yank it off the barbs, throw it in your dive bag or dive tube, and reload for another shot in a very short time before the school of fish swims away. This spear fishing device is the easiest to use, and in many areas of the Mexican coast, Hawaii, and other island areas, it is almost the only type of spearing device used. When I was in Maui, an avid diver working at the Marriot Inn had me show him my spear gun because he had never seen one! You can land even the biggest of fish with a Hawaiian sling, especially if you have the right spear tip on it, but when it comes to the big lingcod, I will only use my spear gun for several reasons.

The spear gun comes in two models, a rubber band–propelled model and a compressed air (pneumatic) model. I much prefer the rubber band model.

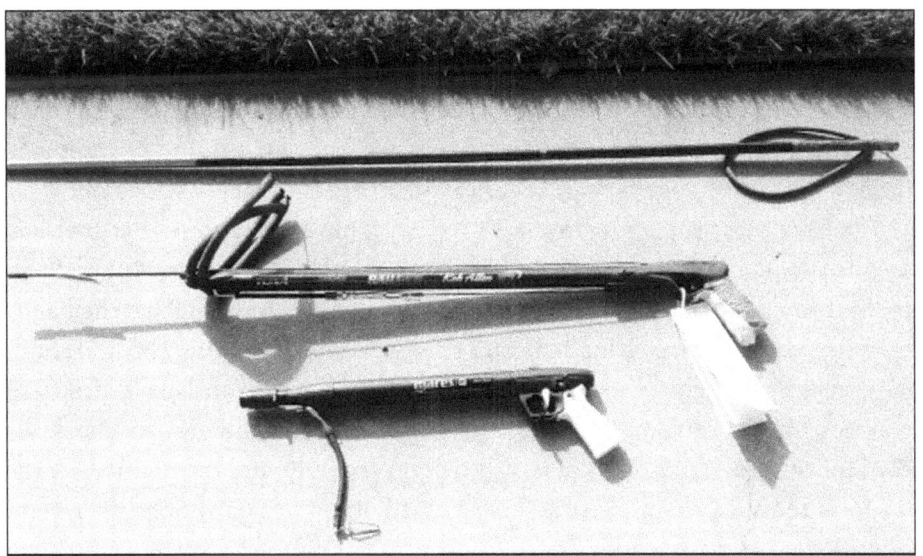

Typical spear gun types

The pneumatic spear gun propels its spear by the air that is compressed into a chamber when you cock the spear into it. This requires a tool that comes with the gun that fits over the tip and has a handle on each side to pull the spear back. Without this tool, cocking is pretty much impossible. So, losing or forgetting this tool, which is usually hanging on a string tied to the gun, puts you out of business. That is one reason I don't like this gun. Another issue that soured me on this type of spear gun is that when I went to get my pneumatic gun for a diving trip in the spring, the salt from the ocean had caused the gun to rust and it was ruined. These are not cheap, and I was truly disappointed; that was the end of my pneumatic spear gun ownership. Also, I didn't like the fact that I was cocking a spear that wasn't going to lock back into a safe position until it was fully cocked, while at any point it had the power to penetrate my skull or my buddy's guts! Disarming it requires you shoot it.

I have to recommend the good ol' trusty rubber band–propelled spear gun. Here, you just push the spear into the gun until it is locked, and only when you pull the rubber band back, or bands if it is the more powerful multi-banded type, and hook the wire on the band into the notch in the spear is it armed and ready to go. Disarming it for safety is as simple as pulling the rubber band back and unhooking it. I do this whenever I am diving near other divers. I only cock my gun when I am ready to shoot because I do not trust the safety mechanism of any spear gun. I have had many fail to work, and the last thing I want is to have to find a way to get a huge spear tip out of my friend's guts or head.

Most of these rubber band spear guns are aluminum, and all that goes bad are the rubber bands, especially if you don't rinse them well after use in saltwater or if you leave them in the sun. It is always a good idea to stretch the bands back like you are going to load the gun before each spear fishing trip and check for cracks in the rubber, just as you should check your fin and mask straps, so you won't have problems with these when you are out fishing. Also, check the cord for rot or wear and that it is still tied on securely, and try to unscrew the tip from the spear to make sure it is screwed on tight. You should always use Loctite on your tip to make sure it stays on, as banging against the rocks when you miss and hitting the hard heads of fish will loosen the tip for sure. All these tips are replaceable, and hence are threaded for removal. Again, check them before each dive and even during your dive because they are expensive.

I like using a gun with two rubber bands for a couple of reasons. One is that in case one breaks, you have a backup. Another is that I like having the extra power on larger fish to stun them good when I shoot them. Especially lingcod, as their mouths are nothing but teeth from their lips to their tonsils—and they will bite! The bands come in various thicknesses and lengths to fit different guns, and each will be easier or more difficult to cock and have more or less power when the trigger is pulled. I usually only cock one band, and I actually have two different thicknesses of bands, so my desired power is even more flexible. I use a small band when I'm shooting small bottom fish on the rocks to keep from dulling my spear tip more than necessary.

Speaking of spear tips, those come in different types as well, and I like different ones for different angling applications. For the smaller fish, I like the "gig" type head that basically looks like your fingers spread out on your hand, with barbs on each finger. Removing the fish is pretty much done by just grabbing the fish and ripping it off the barbs backwards. Always do this when the fish is already in your dive tube or fish bag so you don't lose it. The tip I use for lingcod and larger fish is one that has wings that are folded flat against the spear shaft when entering the fish and then open widely upon the spear moving backwards toward the entry hole. This head will hold about any fish of any size, but it takes substantially more time to remove from the fish. To remove this tip from the fish, you must jam it through the fish until it protrudes out the other side. Then, you fold the wings in against the shaft, slide the little retaining ring over the wing tips to secure them, and then pull the spear back the way it came in. This can be a little tricky with the bulky neoprene gloves of your wetsuit. Again, make sure your fish is secured because when that spear comes out, that fish usually goes nuts!

When spear fishing, I like to set what I call a "chum route." I will find a rock ledge along the shore or an exposed rock formation out from it and swim along an area spreading chum every thirty or forty yards for a couple of hundred yards or less, at a depth that I can see the bottom and the fish that come to eat the chum. Being shallow enough to see the bottom also allows you to navigate from chum pile to chum pile during your hunt. I will then swim back and forth slowly from one end to the other of my chum line for my entire dive, hunting not only the actual chummed area, but the entire area, as the fish will slowly migrate towards the food. Some types of fish, such as the sea trout, also known as kelp greenling, and the perch will move in right away; they are excellent on the dinner table. The Cabazon will move in as well, but slower than the greenlings, and the ling will be the last to the dinner table. I think it is because they are further away and the scent takes longer to reach them, and it takes longer for them to find the bait. Matter of fact, sometimes I find going back the following day to where I chummed can be more productive for lings than that first day. Many times,

I will go to an area that is highly populated with novice abalone divers who take abalone off the rocks that are undersized and then don't replace them properly to the rocks; they become prey to the crab, star fish, seals, and the lingcod. Abalone is the lingcod's dinner of choice, as are the smaller fish that come to the chum!

I will visit that diving spot on a Sunday night or Monday morning after the novices have left and hunt the area hard for lings with great success. I will chum with abalone guts that I glean from the fish cleaning area trashcans, and if I have none of those, I will resort to frozen squid. I also will use my abalone bar to break open sea urchins to spread their guts in the water. The urchins are great for sea trout, black rockfish, China cod, rock crab, and blue rockfish, but they have only secondary value in hunting lingcod and other bottom fish because the urchins are quickly devoured by the greenling and perch. Lingcod, which is my favorite kind of fish to take by spear fishing, prey on other fish, and these other fish are pretty much the mainstay of their diet, so the activity of all these feeding fish can be a draw to the ling. I once speared a sixteen-pound ling that had the head of a three-pound Cabazon in its mouth. It looked through the murky water like a fish with two heads until I swam closer. I speared the ling in the head and landed them both!

When my friends and I spear fish when diving from a boat, we will anchor on an exposed pinnacle out from the shore a ways. These get very little fishing pressure and supply structure for the fish to hang out on. They are like fish magnets, and the lingcod love them. Here, it is a good idea to leave someone in the boat so if the current takes you all out, that person can pick you up. At least leave a long rope dangling and floating three hundred feet or more out of the boat so you can use it as a safety line. The ling here often are swimming actively around the structure as well as lying on the rocks. Near shore, they are almost always stationery on the rocks when you shoot. Still, they will not shy from you. They will often swim right to you or let you dive to within range of them. Here you might take a little longer shot. Also, the ling will be there when you get there, and no chumming or waiting is necessary but can't hurt. Other types of fish are usually abundant on these pinnacles as well. Scuba tanks are handy when diving these pinnacles because many are jetting up from very deep and the fishing is good on these at all depths. When pole fishing from a boat, I always look for such a pinnacle to fish over. Spotting these pinnacles is usually done by finding a patch of kelp growing to the surface from them or from using a depth finder.

When I shoot lingcod and bigger fish, I like to hit them right behind the gills in the upper body and try to damage the spine. I like to shoot and see them convulse while I am getting them in my bag. Hit them too far back in the body, and you have a fight on your hands. One guy I met had an eighteen-pound ling rip twenty-seven stitches worth of gash in his cheek when he hit it too far back and it darted to the end of the rope and turned back at him. He landed it! (Not a sissy!)

Again, I like using two bands on them. So far, my personal record lingcod is twenty-nine pounds, but I am only sixty years old, and before I am ninety or too old to dive, whichever comes later, I plan to break that record! I can't recommend a more fun ocean activity than spear fishing. If you are going to try it, read the article here in my book about abalone diving as well because it discusses how to weight yourself properly for diving, as well as many other free diving tips that you should know. Now, get off the couch and get out there!

How to dive for abalone – an in-depth "how-to-snorkel" lesson, too

Author with Abalone and gear for diving

Diving for abalone is an extremely popular sport on the north coast of California. It is not as hard as most beginning divers make it out to be, and with this lesson, you will know the tricks to making it an easy and enjoyable sport.

Abalone are a saltwater snail that eats kelp and seaweed and lives on rocks near the shore. They have a hard, bowl-shaped shell to protect them, and they attach themselves very firmly to the surface of the rocks with a flat-tissue portion of their body that has a texture of a callous or cow's tongue. The meat is rubbery and must be sliced thinly and pounded with a tenderizer before being fried. Although there are a number of varieties that grow to various sizes, the red abalone is what is common and sought on the north coast of California. These reds must be a minimum of seven inches across any part of the shell to keep, and the record size is about twelve inches. The shells are prized for making jewelry and for other decorative purposes.

Abalone can only be taken by a diver that is holding his or her breath, as no scuba equipment is allowed. Most first-time divers are uncomfortable with this and have such a bad experience that they often give up the sport before they have enough experience to see how simple it is and how fun it can be. Surely, when you don't shoot par on your first round of golf, or even in your entire life, you don't throw in the towel! Just as in any sport, you must persevere along the learning curve until you master just a few techniques that will make your diving experience both pleasurable and productive. Best yet, when you lay that abalone dinner on the table, you will be known as a true snorkeling pro and a culinary genius!

The first trick to making your abalone venture one that you would want to repeat is to pick the right day, and if you are teaching someone to dive for their first time, why ruin that first-time diver's experience by subjecting them to rough waters, very poor visibility, or both. Nothing is worse to the new abalone diver than putting on a bunch of bulky, restrictive, foreign, and awkward gear and jumping into water that heaves you here and yon and dislodges your mask, while the whole time never seeing anything but the top of a piece of bull kelp that startles you by coming in view in one second in the ocean's surge. Everything changes for the new diver when the sea is calm and the visibility is such that he or she can see the bottom while gently floating on the surface. After all, the biggest obstacle that the novice abalone diver must overcome is learning to relax so they can focus on learning how to find the abalone, how to tolerate and address the inevitable water in the mask and snorkel, and getting used to the feel of the rest of the equipment.

Relaxation cannot be stressed enough, as it is the key to both being a successful abalone diver and actually enjoying the sport of ab diving along with spear fishing (which almost every abalone diver eventually takes up). I have written an excellent article on how to spear fish in this book that is a great companion-read to this article. Don't miss it.

Now, becoming relaxed is not something that you meditate into before your dive; it comes mostly from becoming familiar with the ocean, your diving gear, and above all, your actual time spent in the water enjoying the sport. Relaxing allows you the benefits of focusing on your diving techniques, causes you to work much less than the inexperienced diver, which then allows you to breath much easier and calmly, which in turn allows you to dive longer and deeper. Not that diving deep is mandatory to get abalone, as some of the biggest abalone I have ever gotten were taken rock picking in my Levis above the water level at low tide, and there is a great article here in this book on that technique.

The first step of relaxing is realizing that the ocean is not something to be feared, just respected. By that, I mean that every diver's imagination of being eaten by a shark needs to be put into context. For instance, your odds of getting killed in a car wreck on your way to the local grocery store is thousands of times more likely to happen. I have been diving for forty years and I have yet to even personally meet a fellow diver that has even seen a great white shark. So, face the fact that your odds of being bit by a shark are less than your odds of winning the lottery and forget about it! Plus, if you ever do see one, I will share this avoidance technique with you that I use, which is turning the water brown all around me!

When you are diving, you will sometime see curious seals and sea lions that will swim right up to you, often surprising you. This you eventually get used to, and once you stare into their eyes with their long eyelashes and see their curious and friendly demeanor, you kind of enjoy the interaction. This may not be so true when spear fishing, as the hungry little buggers will grab your fish stringer or snag the fish on your spear and get into a tug of war with you, but I have never heard of an actual seal attack.

Another key factor in learning to relax is getting over seasickness. It is hard to relax when you are throwing up. When you are snorkel diving, you will swallow seawater – period. You will also be going up and down and back and forth, and the seaweed and kelp will be washing side to side and up and down at a different pace than you are doing. A lot of movement. If you have ever gotten car sick or air sick, you will be susceptible to getting seasick when you are diving. I know, I get sick real easy! For those that suffer this inherited pitfall, there are a couple of drugs that can help a lot. There are over the counter medicines like the popular Dramamine, which comes in a non-drowsy formula as well as the regular, and another called Bonine; but the best that I have found takes a doctor's visit and comes in the form of a little band-aid-type patch that you place behind your ear called "Trans-derm Scope" or "Scopamine." Trust me, it is worth the cost of the doctor's visit, and you can get enough to take you through the season. While you are there at the pharmacy, pick up some antihistamine as well, as it is handy to keep your sinuses open so you can "clear your ears" when you are diving; the pressure from the water as you dive deeper won't break or harm your eardrums.

Let's speak about this ear-clearing issue for a moment now that you brought it up! Clearing your ears is essential. Not doing so can cause serious ear damage and immense pain. Here is the gist of it. The water weighs a lot, and as you dive deeper, it weighs more. At thirty-three feet it weighs 14.7 pounds more than the 14.7 pounds that was already pushing in on your eardrums from the earth's atmosphere on the shore. Your eardrums are only a little piece of skin-type membrane that is not made to hold the weight of a gallon or two of milk sitting on it. So luckily, your body has these little tubes (estuation tubes) that run from the back of your throat to your inner ear, behind the eardrum, so you can push air out on your ear drum equal to the weight of the water pushing in on it, leaving it in a "neutral weight" state as though nothing were pushing in on it. Without doing this, your eardrum has all that pressure pushing in, stretching it abnormally, and it will eventually tear open. Not good! So as you descend on your dive, whether scuba or free diving, every few feet you should be "equalizing" this pressure by holding your nose and blowing out to "pop" your ears, just like you do when you are coming down from or going up into the mountains. If you cannot clear due to chronic problems or because your sinuses are clogged from allergies or a cold, you should not dive more than five feet in depth. When I dive, I have my hand pushing the rubber of my mask against my nostrils to block them, and I clear my ears about ever four or five feet and once again at the bottom before I begin to work on finding and taking my abalone. Remember, this is not optional, it is essential.

The dangers in the ocean are usually self-inflicted by not using your head. For instance, almost all of the divers that drown, which is the primary cause of death when diving, chose to dive on a day that their experience level was not fit for the ocean conditions. Typically, the diver gets rolled and beaten upon the rocks upon entry or exit from the ocean and knocked unconscious, then drowns. When the ocean is raging rough, find something else fun to do. Go seashell hunting with the kids, hit the local pub, or take a nice stroll and leave diving out. Just because you came to the ocean for the weekend or week doesn't mean you should plan to dive no matter what. This is when respect for the ocean comes into play. Without this respect, you are taking a huge and unacceptable, foolish, risk.

One thing that I see a lot is that when newer divers are introduced to a particular diving spot, they insist on using it whether rough or not because it is the only one they know about, while right around the corner is another cove that is calm that day due to the direction of the surf, loaded with just as many abalone, and has just as easy an access. Scouting such spots is a great way to spend a day when the ocean is rough. Also, another hint is to look at certain areas at low tide. Many times when the tide goes out, rock formations are exposed further seaward of a cove that act as a jetty, breaking the surf outside and leaving the cove calm and very diveable even when the ocean is somewhat rough. But know one thing, the ocean has many days that you just cannot safely dive it. One of those days is when it is dead calm and you have a third-degree hangover or are sick or tired for any reason. Wait until you feel better. The coast is a beautiful place and made to enjoy, so why take the risk? If in doubt at all, hit the pub or the bowling alley!

The most common mistake a new abalone diver makes is diving in water that is too shallow. The ocean almost always has some surge to it that sweeps you around like a washing machine. When you dive down in six or eight feet of water, by the time you fine an abalone, you are ten feet away from it or out of air from fighting and kicking to stay in one place long enough to pry the ab off. You also run the risk of bumping your head, which we spoke of above, along with becoming more seasick than you can imagine. When you get in a little deeper water, there is little or no noticeable surge. When I am diving, I like about fifteen to twenty feet of sea below me. Here, I don't kick or swim at all while waiting for a dive, which lets me relax and rest and breathe to build the oxygen in my blood for the next dive. Many new divers feel that they don't have the "air" to dive this deep when in fact this takes much less air than what is used fighting the surge in the shallow water. This is something that every diver that continues this sport will learn as he or she becomes more relaxed and comfortable in the ocean environment. Here again, learning this is best done on a day when the water is clearer so the diver can see the bottom. Later, you will become so relaxed and comfortable that you will leave the surface into a greyness and become fine with the bottom coming into focus once you have reached a depth of ten or more feet. You will then come to recognize that the ocean floor is still the same old ocean bottom as when it was clear and the abalone are still under the same old rocks as always. Nothing new!

Another mistake made by divers is improperly weighting themselves. To explain briefly, weights are required when diving to offset the buoyancy of your wetsuit. Face it, the wetsuit is a layer of highly buoyant foam rubber designed to keep you warm. It will not allow you to sink unless you are weighted down to counteract its floatation characteristics. Hence, you must wear a weight belt that is somewhat awkward and heavy for certain, which you will soon learn when you are hiking up a steep ocean bluff with your dive tube full of abalone and fish and this twenty-pound (plus or minus) burden. So, what is the right weight? The answer is that amount of weight that makes you feel like you would diving in a pool with nothing but your swimsuit on. Let's call this "neutral buoyancy," as it is known in the diving world. Sounds easy in theory, but it may be eighteen pounds or twenty-five pounds, like what I wear (more if I have scuba tanks on). Well, the answer depends on things like the thickness of your wetsuit, how big your love handles are, and your personal preference for weighting as you become more experienced. But I learned a trick that works for everyone when I was in the Navy Seals' diving school in Subic Bay, Philippines. When you are choosing your weighting amount, which will stick with you for most of your diving career unless you change to a much heavier or lighter wetsuit, take the following little amount of time so as to begin your diving on the proper note. Start with about twenty pounds of weight and go in the saltwater, not freshwater, as the buoyancy is different, and float with your hands to your sides. Then you either add or subtract weight so that when floating idle, in a straight up and down position, the water level is such that when you are looking out of your mask, you are looking at half above the water and half below.

Put another way, the water level is halfway up your mask when you are floating without moving. This is perfect. This will allow you to float with ease on the water as you rest between dives but allow you to descend easily without fighting the buoyancy and using your precious oxygen for no reason. Again, it is another factor in your overall relaxation.

When you dive, use a dive tube. It is an inner tube covered with a canvas covering with zippers and straps so you can transport your gear to and from the diving spot on your back. It is a place for you to keep your abalone and, most importantly, it is your best pal if you get a cramp, get seasick, tired, or need to rest. It is also a great place to take a break and shoot the breeze with your fellow divers! If you are also spear fishing or gathering urchins and crab for your sushi feed at the campground, take a dive bag for those and clip it to your tube, as the fish fins and urchin spines will puncture your tube and you will be spending money for another. Also, don't over-inflate your tube. You will have less room to put stuff, and it makes you work harder to reach over it to put stuff in and take stuff out when you're diving, and it's also more difficult to climb on for your resting or B.S. session with your buddies. Put in just enough air to keep it above water so your game doesn't fall out when you grab it while you are swimming around.

Finding the abalone seems tricky to some beginning divers, but very soon they stand out like a sore thumb. They are the color of the sea bottom, and like rocks, many have corals and kelp on their shells, but once you become relaxed you can see them as though they were on your picnic table. They are on the rocks, not in the sand. Just give yourself time. Diving on a clear day with an experienced friend helps, too. Many times I will dive down in ten feet of water and look up to my "student" and point at an abalone with my finger while looking up at him or her. But, to get the nicest abalone, you have to look under the rocks. The abalone are delicacies sought after by every predator in the ocean. They like to hide upside down under rocks, in crevasses, and in beds of seaweed. When you dive down, plan to look upside down, which is about impossible in shallow water due to the surges that we talked about earlier. When you find one, try to ascertain if it is legal in size before you start to take it, as these gastropods are very fragile and will die easily if you damage them in any way. So try to avoid touching them unless you truly believe they are "keepers" so we can preserve the resource. I don't mean to measure it with your abalone gauge that every diver is required to carry, I just mean that you should overcome your excitement long enough to assess the size visually, knowing that your mask works as a "magnifier." The experienced diver will seldom make this mistake. If you do take a small one, take the time to place it back on the rocks where it is safe from predators because it takes it some time to re-attach and get re-oriented to protect itself. Putting it back where it came from is best, but if you can't do that, at least put it in a crevasse or somewhere protected. Many new divers just measure them and drop them from the surface if they are too small, which is very poor sportsmanship. I will mention here too that it is important, and legally required, that the tip of your abalone pry bar be dull and only 1/8th inch in thickness so as not to cut the abalone that you are taking so it may live on if it is undersized. I have had game wardens enter the campground and inspect every diver's bar!

Again, abalone are snails, gastropods, if you will. They attach themselves to the rocks with their "foot." Your job is to slide your abalone bar between this foot and the rock to be able to pry them from the rock. In deeper waters, where the water is calm, or on calmer days, they relax because they don't have to worry about getting torn from the rocks by the water surge and their shell is an inch or two above their foot and the rock. If they sense movement in their area, or get touched, they immediately close their shell tightly to the rock to protect themselves. So it is key that you "sneak" up on them and methodically place your bar between them and the rock, insert it, and then pry them off if needed. Many times just this insert is enough to free them from the rock. If you find one closed to the rock and clinging on for dear life, go to another one (unless it is that record one you are after and willing to spend some time on), as that one has already been pried on and there is a good chance of not getting it but still causing it lethal damage. Don't worry about one particular abalone because, as you will see, there are plenty more.

Remember, you are only down a few feet, a second or two from the surface, and there is no need to rush and tense up. Relax and take your time. When you dive, just flip over and lift one leg into the air and let its weight push you down; when that foot enters the water, give it one kick, and what do you know? You are already down over ten feet! Don't use your arms as they are of little help;

just kick slowly and evenly with your fins and you will have all the power you need. When you ascend, look up for kelp or other obstacles so you can avoid them and you will be fine. Always take a friend or two with you for safety. If the water gets rough or you begin to cramp or tire, swim in immediately. Watch for boats and watercraft and use a bright dive tube for this reason. If you are ever caught in a rip tide, just relax and go with it and swim sideways to it, not against it. It will let you go soon and not suck you down, and you can go to shore another route. And always remember, as a last resort, you can pull the quick release on your weight belt and let it drop to the bottom, then you couldn't sink if you tried to! This greatly reduces your maneuverability and rules out any further diving, but it is a lifeboat that you have at your fingertips. Now, relax, have fun, and be safe!

How to dive for sea urchins for sushi – get your very own free "uni"

Sea Urching, AKA "Uni" in the sushi bar

This article is about how to get sea urchins for sushi when you are at the ocean. In order to gather sea urchins, you must dive or snorkel for them. There are smaller urchins exposed on the rocks at low tide, but these are typically not big enough to eat. Finding sea urchins big enough to eat is usually done in water that is from ten to fifty feet deep. I do dive with scuba equipment sometimes, but most of the time I use a snorkel and free dive by holding my breath when I am getting sea urchins. Usually, I am killing three birds with one stone, as I am also abalone diving and spear fishing when I gather urchins. I seldom go after just one thing because I am donning my dive gear anyway and they are all found in the same place, so why not! I use a float tube for my abalone and fish and carry a separate bag for my urchins so they can hang on the float and not poke holes in my dive tube.

The urchins have needle-sharp spines that stick out from their shells everywhere on their bodies. They protrude out two or three inches and are barbed similar to a porcupine quill, so if you do get spines in you, they don't come out easily. They are painful and they are brittle and can easily snap off in you, which is a problem. I spent thousands on my index finger to remove several from when my hand slipped off my abalone bar as I was breaking the urchins open to chum for fish. I had to go under anesthesia and have the entire finger laid open to the bone and cleaned out. I made the mistake of waiting too long to go to the doctor, and I almost lost my finger. Now the first knuckle is permanently twice the size of my other index finger and has been that way for twenty years! Moral of the story is to be careful. Use diving gloves, and even then handle with care because the spines will go right through them easily. I had mine on when I was injured. When you pick them up, hold them loosely and gently and be careful putting them into your bag. The commercial urchin divers have a metal claw in one hand that sticks out about sixteen inches in front of their hand, and they rake them into a canvas bag. Diving without scuba tanks and having to go up for air and to drop the sea urchins into your bag between each urchin doesn't lend itself to using such a tool. Your air needs limit the time you have to get the urchins, so you have a tendency to act a little hastier than you should. So safety is a key element to take to heart as you learn how to gather sea urchins.

The sea urchins live on the rocks at the bottom of the ocean and like to be in crevasses and in areas that are somewhat protected from the surge of the surf when they are in the shallower water. When you are in an area that has urchins, there are usually a lot of them. But sometimes you will find a little patch of them with ten or twenty in the same area. When I am diving, I usually don't go looking for them. I just take them when I see them in my travels. The sea urchins attach themselves to the rocks with the smaller spines underneath. They are not firmly attached, but you are not going to just reach down and grab one. I use my abalone bar or spear gun tip to "flick" them loose. Once they are loose, I grasp them ever so lightly with both hands, almost just balancing them within my two hands so that they are almost floating freely as I carry it up to the bag. The bag that I use has two metal handles that can be propped wide open so the urchin can just be dropped in the bag. If the spines get stuck and the urchin doesn't go to the bottom, shake the bag to cause it to go down inside further. Definitely don't push it with your hand! As you gather sea urchins, keep an eye out for rock crab because they smell the damaged urchins and come looking for food — they are a great-tasting meal themselves. You just can't be too much of a sissy to pick them up while they are holding those big giant claws up at you!

Now, when you swim back to shore and hike back to the truck, safety should be your top concern. Don't let the waves wash you onto the sea urchins, don't throw them over your shoulder, and don't fall on them when you are hiking back. At camp or at your house, keep them away from kids and pets and where no one will accidently bump into them. Also, when you are breaking them open to get to the roe, which is the part you eat, called uni at the sushi bar, be careful. I use a real long knife that I lay blade down on top of it and tap it lightly, but firmly, with a hammer or meat pounder to split the shell in half. I will use another knife or long fork to separate the two halves of the shell enough to scoop the uni out with a spoon. Remember to dispose of the discarded shells safely as well so no accidents occur. Break out the sushi rice, serve the orange slimy urchin roe, and gross your kids out along with most of the adults! I like to say that sea urchins taste like the ocean smells. I love them!

Fishing with hooks when diving – bet you never heard of doing this before

I was over at the ocean for a fishing, abalone-diving, and spear-fishing trip last year, and one morning while sitting on the john, I had an epiphany. For some reason, this is where I usually have such life-changing brainstorms.

I had been out abalone diving the day before, got my three ab, and decided to do a little spear fishing because the ocean water had cleared up enough to see a remarkably good distance. By this, I mean that I could see the bottom of the ocean in about twenty feet of water. That is great visibility for the north coast of California because many days are between five and eight feet, which makes the spear fishing almost impossible.

I had brought some chum with me from the cleaning station at the campground that day, which consisted of abalone guts and pieces of leathery trimmings from the body. The guts are great fish bait. They have some consistency to them from the outer membrane, but they are full of digested seaweed or some sea plant that seems to really spread throughout the seawater and attracts the fish for a distance. I think the fish are actually attracted to the smell of the digestive fluids in the guts, rather than the seaweed itself. However, the guts are soft and they are swallowed by the fish of all sizes pretty readily and disappear as fish bait quickly. The larger chunks of the abalone body are not easily swallowed by the littler fish and seem to be liked more by the larger ones like Cabazon, lingcod, and the kelp greenling, which are my favorite fish to catch and eat. The abalone meat is nearly as tough as leather, which is why it is necessary to cut it thin and pound it when you are cooking it. This comes in handy when using it as fish bait because it stays on the hook no matter how much the little fish nibble and jerk on it. Matter of fact, it stays on the hook until it is well down in the fish's "engine room" when he swallows it! For this reason, if you are fishing the ocean with abalone meat as bait, it is best to make sure you thread the hook all the way through the bait so that the barbs are fully exposed or you may not be able set the hook into the fish so that the barb can do its job.

Anyway, the water was more clear than usual, and this was causing the fish to dart away when I dove down to my bait pile to get a shot with my spear gun. The clearer the ocean water, the spookier the fish are. I caught a few fish, or I should say speared, but some lunkers got away from me. To get the fish I did get, I would stay well off to the side of the chum piles and dive to the bottom away from the bait where the fish were feeding. I would then slither along the bottom over the rocks and among the kelp and sea grass to the chum and carefully place my spear gun into position and put the spear appropriately through the fish heads! Even this approach scared most of the fish away, but it was a heck of a lot better fishing with this method than diving down over the top of the fish like a giant space ship blocking the sun from the fishes' world.

I didn't do too bad fishing that day, but I really had to work and, for the most part, I got the smaller and dumber fish instead of the huge fish that I was after.

Now back to the toilet and my epiphany.

I love fishing from the shore of the ocean when I am at the coast, so I always have my fishing tackle close at hand. I got the idea of using large fishing weights and real heavy line with large fishhooks to fish those same elusive fish that I am after when I am diving. There are usually many fish where I dive because I try to stay away from the shore where the shore fishermen can cast so I am in an area that isn't fished out. This is also nice because it avoids getting tangled up in all the monofilament fishing line that is abundant from those bank fishermen getting snagged in the rocks every third cast!

I decided to build and take these little fishing rigs out for a try. I tied only two feet of eighty-pound spider wire to a one-pound fishing sinker and tied the other end to a one-ought hook. I baited them with the abalone guts and some squid I had and spread them over a fifty-yard area along a rock outcropping so they were easy to find when I wanted to check them. Surprisingly enough, over the day every line led to a couple of fish each!

I couldn't find anything in the fishing regulations about such a fishing technique, so I kind of made up my own from the information that I gleaned there-in. Hopefully, there is some sort of statute of limitations on fish and game violations if I did in fact violate the law and one of our finest fish and game wardens is reading this article. Matter of fact, this was actually a friend of mine that was on the crapper who had this epiphany! The fishing regulations said I could have two poles with up to three hooks per line, so that is what I did, except for the fishing pole, and I used six hooks on six different weights. I was surprised at how effective this was, although it was a little awkward trying to bait hooks and remove hooks from fish with my bulky diving gloves on. Of course, you need a measuring device because the various types of fish have different size limits that you must obey. I have a dive tube, which is an inner tube that has a canvas covering that fits over it and a zipper to enclose it to put my fish in. I also usually attach a netted fish bag or spear fishing dive stringer to it for the fish that have sharp fins, like perch and blue rockfish, that will poke holes in the tube.

I came back that day with most of my limit of bottom fish, a few ocean perch, four nice abalone (the limit is three now), some rock crab that were drawn to the chum, and a few sea urchins (uni) for some sushi! I could barely carry my bag full of fish and seafood up the hill! All the people at the camp were thrilled to see me return with their seafood dinner over my shoulders! My new idea worked, but I haven't been back to try it again yet. I may go over to the coast, which is about five hours from my house, and give it a whirl again. This was a blast! And don't get me wrong, I was spear fishing the whole time I was fishing with the set lines, too. I have never heard of anyone but me trying this type of fishing, but I am sure glad I discovered the technique!

Octopus story – an exciting diving safety lesson I wanted to share with you

Giant Pacific Octopus that can grow to over 20 feet

Let me tell you a story about a time I almost drowned while spear fishing so you can see that you have to always respect the ocean and everything in it!

The most stupid thing that I ever did while spear fishing, without a doubt, was attempting to spear and land a twenty-foot giant pacific octopus when I was free diving by myself in Northern California in Mendocino County. Bad enough that I was in the ocean snorkeling by myself in the first place, but this is something I often do because I am usually at the coast by myself, or the other divers I am with are either too tired or hung over for diving. I love to abalone dive and hunt lingcod, Cabazon, and other rockfish, so it is either dive alone or sit on the bank with a fishing pole. Don't get me wrong, I love that, too, but I do that on the days that the ocean is simply too rough for diving or I am tired or hung over!

The day of this event was a beautiful sunny day, and the ocean was calm and pretty clear. I had about fifteen feet of visibility, which was quite a change from the ocean's normal murkiness of only six to ten feet of visibility, so I was excited about being able to see far enough to spearfish. I had been out for a couple of hours, and I was heading in when I spotted something white about twelve feet down in about twenty-five feet of water. This struck me as kind of odd because you see stuff on the bottom and you see white plastic bags and such floating on the top of the water, but not often midway between.

I swam over to check it out, and I couldn't find what I had seen earlier. I knew I was in the exact area, so I was somewhat stumped. I made a dive down to the depth of what I saw and was looking around in the bull kelp to see if I could find the object. The ocean's waves were gently causing the bull kelp to sway to and fro about five feet every few seconds. As the kelp washed up to me while I was on this dive, I noticed the white thing once again right in front of me just two feet away. I looked at it and saw the unmistakable suction cups on the tentacle of an octopus' arm. The arm was huge! I followed it up and there was this octopus head that was bigger than mine, and his eye was peering at me from just two feet away!

Octopi are invisible when on the ocean floor and on kelp because their outer bodies are camouflaged exactly like the rocks and seaweed in the ocean. Only their undersides are snow white, and it is a rare occasion that an octopus will allow that white to be exposed. Only the ocean's movement had caused it to turn up from the kelp from time to time, in this case.

I do not know what got into my head! I swam up to my dive tube and unlatched my spear pole from the hook. I had left my spear gun at home, and all I had was this Hawaiian sling spear pole about six feet long. I carefully watched from the surface as the octopus drifted back and forth with the current. I got the pole loose and got a few needed breaths in me. I developed this plan, which looking back was borderline insane. I figured I would just dive down and spear the octopus in the head, and with my body's momentum from kicking hard with my fins, rip him neatly from the twenty-foot long bull kelp stalk. Then, with my spear pole pointed upward, I would take him up to my dive tube and simply swim in the hundred yards to the bank with him wrapped around me and the float tube and go show him off!

Stupid idea.

I took a deep breath, while still being somewhat drained from holding it from the last dive. I stretched the rubber band as far as I could on the Hawaiian sling and down I went. Damn if I couldn't see him, until all of a sudden he floated right to me, and that arm turned over again, and I looked up and there was his head. I had already been holding my breath quite a while and was approaching the end of this dive, but I thought I would lose him if I waited, so I let him have it with the spear pole. Then I kicked with my fins, using all my might, and ripped as hard as I could with my arms. I managed to free about three of his eight arms, each ten feet, which were probably already free or I wouldn't have even got those. He didn't budge, and had he wrapped any one of those arms around any part of my body, I would not be telling you this story today.

Now, with my body already beginning to want air, I began my new Plan B that I developed there on the spot, which was not much better than Plan A, which had already failed. I had torn his head open a bit with my huge yank on the spear, so I then inserted my fingers from each hand into the hole and ripped an even larger hole that my whole hand would fit in. I reached in and began grabbing anything and everything in his head and yanking it out. I did this about five times, and my body had begun to gasp for air against my closed mouth. I had to get to the surface! I yanked my spear out of his head and re-shot him in the thick, meaty, arm to try to hold him on the barbs of my spear. I went towards the surface, holding the spear pole by the end of the rubber band, and had my arm outstretched as far as possible, but my snorkel was still about a foot from the surface of the ocean. I had to surface, and when I did I felt the barbs pull loose from the meat of the octopus. There was nothing I could do. I gasped in about six or eight breaths of air that my body was desperate for, which was not nearly enough to satisfy its needs, and back down I went. I couldn't find that octopus anywhere. I came up and got a few more breaths and down I went, over and over, searching every piece of bull kelp in that forest. He had gotten away, but I knew he was dead somewhere close.

The water was twenty-five feet deep, and I was exhausted from the previous long dive, as remember. I was on my way in to shore when this all occurred! I couldn't see the bottom from the surface, so I had to dive pretty deep to try and find him. I dove for over three more hours straight, searching for him, and even came back the next day as I figured his dead body would be upturned and out of his hiding spot, but to no avail. I had nearly drowned and I lost him. As I said, had he gotten any one of those arms that I ripped loose around any part of my body, I would not be writing this story today! I know this now because one time I speared a ten-foot octopus, and getting him free from the rocks took both me and my dive partner. This was by far the most crazy and the most dangerous, idiotic, stupid, imbecile, insane, ignorant, un-smart, foolish, asinine, fool hearted, mentally deranged thing I have ever done while snorkeling and free diving. I won't do anything that stupid again—although last time out (by myself) I decided to spear a seven-foot mouth full of dangerous teeth known as a wolf eel, but by the time I got my spear gun loose from my float tube, he had vanished or I would probably be missing too many fingers to type this! But I promise — maybe — not to do anything stupid again!

Ten best safety tips for diving – this could save your life

1. Go with a buddy. Matter of fact, the more buddies, the safer you are. And stay close.

2. Bring a dive tube or other floatation device. Dropping your weight belt is a last resort.

3. Check your gear before diving—fin straps, mask straps, hook up—and test your regulator.

4. Do not dive if you are tired, ill, hung over, or impaired from medication or drugs.

5. Do not underestimate the ocean's conditions – it can always get rougher quick.

6. Do not enter the water where it is too rough and can slam you against the rocks.

7. Pay attention when you are descending and ascending, watch for snags and traps.

8. Return to the shore if you become tired, cramped, or seasick.

9. Swim sideways to rip tides; they will let you loose soon, and you can get in elsewhere.

10. Pay attention to the ocean's incoming waves when you are exiting or entering the ocean.

OTHER OCEAN FISHING AND FUN

Fishing for rockfish from shore

Author's daughter fishing with dad on the north coast of California

Fishing the ocean in from shore can be tricky and dangerous, but can be easy and fun, along with safe, if you follow a few guidelines, tricks, and hints that are included in this article. Although beach fishing is shore fishing, too, this article is about fishing for rockfish from the rocky areas of the ocean because that is my main interest and what I have had the most success with.

The gear and tackle needed for shore fishing is pretty simple and inexpensive. I use a pretty hefty rod that is not expensive and about seven feet long or longer, with a reel that will accommodate about thirty-pound test line and cast easily. I use hooks that are cheap and three-ounce weights. I don't use tobacco sacks that are sold as a cheap substitute for weights that you add rocks to, as they are swept around too much by the surf and cause a lot of snags. The hooks I use are any medium size, like you would use for channel catfish, carp, or black bass. Because of all the snags on the kelp and rocks, I never waste the money on a leader or swivels. I just tie the weight on bottom and make two loops in the line to hold the two hooks about eighteen inches apart, with the lowest one being about eighteen inches from the weight. Plan on being patient and re-rigging quite often because this is part of the game and you might as well accept it. Don't hurry and be happy!

As far as bait goes, there are many choices. My favorites are mussels, abalone guts (from the garbage cans in campgrounds in Northern California), squid from the store, and the little crabs and creatures that live in the mussel beds on the rocks. I make it a point to gather mussels first thing at low tide when I am at the ocean because that is the only time they are exposed and available. Even then, if the ocean is raging, you can't get them without risking being washed off the rocks by a sleeper wave – a huge wave that is much larger than the rest, coming by surprise. There is a section about getting mussels for dinner here in this fine fishing book for you, too! Once I get the mussels, I like to either steam them a little or microwave them slightly to firm them up and get their shells to open, or they are a hassle to get out of their shells. I find that the fish could care less that they are cooked a little and they bait up and stay on the hook ten times better. Always yank the biggest mussels off the rock that you can because they are best for baiting. The mediums are best for your tummy, but you can only usually eat them between the months of October and March while the water is cold and there is no "red tide" present. If I can't get mussels for some reason, I buy squid. Look in the fish market and see if there are fresh ones by chance, but frozen ones will do.

Fishing from the rocks in North California

I like to fish when the tide is about halfway on its way out. That way, you can follow the water and move outward on the rocks you are fishing from as the tide goes out and move in with it as it comes in. If the sea is raging, opt for a real high cliff and just drag your fish ungracefully up the cliff face with your thirty-pound test because this is much better than dying by being swept off the rocks. You can also fish the cliffs at high tide when the water below is a little deeper. I like to find a little cove that is calm due to a rock formation, one that becomes exposed at low tide out in front of the cove that breaks all the surf from it. Sometimes it will be a little chute or inlet that is exposed at low tide and is calm. Some days the water is just flat and opportunities are wide open for spots, but never take your eye off the ocean because about every ten thousandth wave is a sleeper, they say. Also, don't travel out to your desired spot and get trapped out on the rocks by the incoming tide that swallows your exit while you aren't paying attention. This happens very easily.

Just like about anywhere, the fishing is best where fewer people fish, so the more you are willing to hike or climb hills to fishing holes, the better you will do. Always take a friend with you for safety's sake when possible and carry your cell phone, too. It's the ocean, so plan on a cool breeze and dress appropriately so you can enjoy yourself without discomfort. A snack and drink come in handy, too, in case the fish are biting and you stay longer than you planned. I use a small backpack instead of a tackle box and carry a plastic bag or two for the fish to go in before they go in the pack. I also carry binoculars, and seldom do I not have some great reason to use them.

The fish you can catch vary from perch, Cabazon, lingcod, kelp greenling, China cod, black and blue rockfish, and even a rock crab from time to time. Some people use a pole with a treble hook tied to it with a foot-long wire and poke it into the holes under rocks, catching all these same fish and eels as well; this is called "poke polling" and is fun for folks of all ages! If you are going to the ocean, it is a must-do activity!

Catching surfperch off of the beach

Surfperch fishing from beaches is a great way to have some fun at the ocean while the family is enjoying the beach. I mostly like to fish from the rocks when I am at the ocean, but I will never turn down a day of beach fishing when I am there. The rubber lip, red tail, shiner, silver, and barred perch are the main fish that you will catch when surf fishing. You will run across the occasional stingray and even a shark once in a while, as well as crab, but you mostly catch surfperch when fishing on the beach, from my experience. The lingcod, Cabazon, and other bottom fish like to hang out in the rocky areas. Flounders live in the sand but are usually out further than where you can cast.

Catching surfperch requires small hooks like you would use for cat fishing. The surf-fishing rig is a setup with a weight on the bottom and two hooks above it. The lower hook I put about three feet above the weight and the other hook about eighteen inches above that. I make a loop with the line and tie the loop into a knot to make the loop where I attach the hook. No swivel or tackle is required because I tie the fishing weight right to the line. Nice and cheap! The weight I use depends on how rough the ocean is, but is usually only a few ounces because I only use about eight- to twelve-pound test line, and I like to cast hard to get my bait out as far as possible.

I like to use shrimp or squid for bait for surfperch, and I choose squid first because it stays on the hook better. You can use the little crab and creatures that you can get by digging on the beach or in mussel beds on the rocks; they are all excellent for catching surfperch. Some folks use mussels, and I hear some fishermen even use night crawlers, which I have never tried. I have used abalone pieces when I was over at the coast on an abalone diving trip and they seemed to work okay as well.

When I am fishing for surfperch, I like to cast out as far as possible with a nice long surf-fishing rod. This long surf-fishing rod's main benefit is that when you set it up to watch it on the beach, the line stays out of the waves that are washing against the shore so you can see your bites. This is why you should have a little heavier weight on your line when the ocean is a little rougher, to keep the line spanned over these breaking waves. Your fishing rod tip will still move with the waves, but if your line isn't in the direct break of the waves and is just where the water is rolling up and down, it is easy to tell the surfperch bites from the action of the waves. The surfperch bite is that familiar quick series of jerks that looks just like the classic fish bite, and you can see it amongst all the movement of your pole. If you can pick your pole up and feel it, then by all means, set the hell out of the hook like with any fish!

Once you catch them, you will need to know how to clean surfperch. If they are larger than a pound and a half or two pounds, I will fillet them like other fish. For the smaller ones, I just scrape the scales off, cut off their heads, and gut them as I would a bluegill, worrying about the bones when I am eating them.

You can go fishing for surfperch any time of year, although they breed in the winter months and come near shore in numbers both then and when they come in to lay their live babies from mid-spring to midsummer, and the fishing for surfperch is better during these times. In essence, that gives you from about November to July to get into them good, so that is quite a generous season. There is a limit on them, so make sure you check the rules out so you don't catch that thousand-dollar extra perch!

Getting mussels off the rocks at low tide for chowder and fishing bait

Author getting mussels off the rocks at low tide for mussel chowder and steamed mussels

This section is about how to get mussels off the rocks at the ocean, how to clean and prepare mussels for cooking, and how to steam them the best way for eating. There isn't a lot to getting mussels, but without having a few tools and a little basic knowledge, it can be somewhat intimidating. With the information here in this article, you will find yourself admired as an old pro at gathering mussels!

When we go camping at the ocean for our abalone diving trips, the first thing I do is gather mussels, if they are in season, and make a batch of mussel chowder that is around for days. I say in season because here in Northern California we have what they call a "red tide," which causes the mussels to have a toxic bacteria of some sort in them that can be very dangerous to people, so they put up warning signs not to eat them. The legal season is actually year round, so you can still get them for fishing bait, and mussels are great fishing bait. I will microwave them until they firm up and the shells pop open; this way, they are easy to get out of the shell and stay on the hook better. The fish bite them just as well cooked a little as they do raw.

To get mussels, you need to have a sharp and rigid knife and a five-gallon bucket to put them in. The mussels attach themselves to the rocks and to each other with strong, hairlike, fibrous strands that must be cut to remove them. Mussels live on rocks that are right at the surf line in the ocean, where the waves crash onto them, and their life depends on these fibers withstanding this surf. They are strong. It is possible to just rip them off if you can grip them well enough (have gloves so you don't tear up your hands on broken shells and rocks) and if you don't mind working your rear off! I highly recommend using a knife to remove mussels from the rocks so you can claim to be sane if anyone is watching! When you slice the "hairs" that hold them, they come right off.

The mussels grow in big beds, usually on nearly flat rocks where they are often exposed during lower tides. They are not a deep-water creature and seldom do you see them even five feet underwater unless it is a high tide. I have been spear fishing and abalone diving around these mussel beds for years and this is a fact. They are typically found in huge beds with thousands of them or even millions growing almost on top of each other, and so thick that you are walking on them every step when you are looking for the size that you are after. As I mentioned, when the ocean is rough, the waves pound these rocks and wash over them with great force. You do not go on these rocks for any reason when the ocean is rough if you value your life! Even when the ocean is calm, you still must keep a diligent watch on the ocean, as about every ten thousandth wave is a freak, they say, which can sweep you away before you know it. Even ankle-deep water washing with such force can sweep your feet from under you and can be very dangerous. This is especially true for kids. Keep your eye out for a highly protected mussel bed that can be your private and safe honey hole every time you gather mussels.

The size you are after depends on what you are going to do with them and what you have in mind when you are preparing mussels for eating. If I am making chowder, I like the big ones because they can be cut in nice chunks. For steaming them in the shell, I like a medium size, and for fish bait, I like as big as I can get. My dad and I used to can them with a little olive oil, liquid smoke, jalapeño peppers, and garlic, and for that we used a size between the biggest and medium sized. When we fried them like oysters in seasoned breadcrumbs, we would use the giants and cut them in half before we breaded and fried them. I may as well mention that we would always steam or microwave the mussels to open them for cooking them these other ways to make the job easy.

When you clean your mussels and while you gather them, keep your eye out for ones that are dead and filled with sand. They look alive, are heavy, and can be easily mistaken for good mussels; if you put them in your steaming pot, the boiling water will free the sand and your meal will be ruined, unless you like chewing on sand! This is very important; When you are cleaning the mussels, take each one in the sink or under the faucet and rinse it thoroughly with your hands and double check if it's alive. Tap the mussel against another one or with a knife handle and you will learn to recognize the hollow "thunk" of the dead and hollow ones. Rinse all the sand off and pull off the remaining pebbles that are attached to the fibers. Then the mussels are ready to cook.

Many people just don't know how to steam mussels. Most importantly, you do not use water! You put a tad of olive oil in the bottom of a huge pot and get it hot. Throw in a cube of butter that is cut into six chunks so it melts quickly and throw in a handful of chopped garlic. Brown the garlic and keep an eye on it so you don't burn it. Nothing tastes better than browned garlic or worse than burnt garlic. Burning garlic is a sign that you do not have a clue what the hell you are doing when it comes to cooking and you need to go knit potholders for a real cook or something! Before the garlic is browned, throw in a handful or two of chopped parsley. Rather than turn the fire down when the garlic is just right, you are going to stop the heat by dumping in a half of a bottle of white wine to cool things down. Use good white wine. Chardonnay is a good choice, and I did say "good," not that cheap, sour, two-dollar stuff you switch into expensive empty bottles to serve your friends when they dine with you! Don't use a sweet wine like Riesling or a tart one like Gewürztraminer (however you pronounce the damn stuff!). Red wine is way too overwhelming; however, it makes a good choice for serving with the meal. Heat the wine back to a boil and turn the fire down just a little, but keep it boiling and cover the pot. When all the mussels are wide open, they are done! There is no risk of burning the garlic now because it is buried in wine, seawater, and the juices that are released from within the mussels when they open during the steaming process. This juice is what makes the meal, and each person should be served a dipping bowlful so they can dip their sourdough bread in it and scoop it with the mussel shells to slurp in with the mussel. It is the best part, and it just gets better every day like a good pasta sauce. Hold on, I'm starting to talk like an Italian, and I'm an Okie Irishman!

We like to spread newspaper out on our whole table in several layers and just toss the shells aside on the paper as we go. When we are done eating, we put the garbage can by the end of the table, fold the newspaper up, slide it all in one motion into the can, and the table is clean! We do the same when we are eating crawdads, and this is the only way to go. If you come to my house and you are expecting some formal sit-down affair, you are in for a huge surprise, and I don't care who you are! You may find yourself drinking out of a mason jar, and the language can get quite colorful! Just be grateful that we aren't passing gas until we get to know you good enough halfway through the meal!

Clam digging with your homemade clam pump

The author using his home made clam pump at low tide

If any of you sportsmen or women are even thinking about trying the sport of clam digging, you need to learn how to build a clam pump or you are in for a lot of work. Pumping clams with a clam pump is about a hundred times easier and faster than every other method that I have seen, all of which usually involve that archaic device known as a shovel. There is no need for such a dreaded tool when the clam pump is deployed! The clams I am talking about here are horsenecks, geoducks, Washingtons, softshells, and that type of long-necked clam.

Soft shelled clam

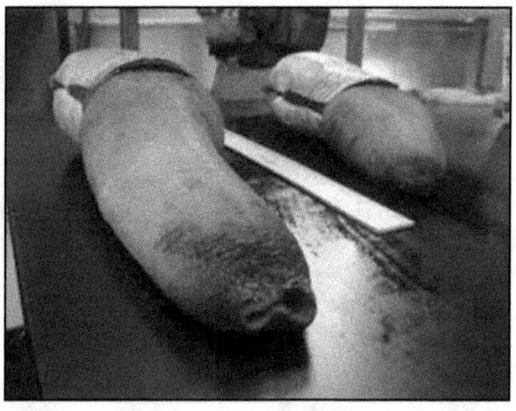

Goeduck Clam

The clam pump is a simple device and can be made easily in your garage at home at very little expense. All you need is a thirty-inch piece of three-inch pvc pipe with a flat, glue-on cap for one end of it; this is for the body of the pump.

Then you need a thirty-inch-long piece of quarter-inch rod that is threaded for about three inches on each end, this will hold a handle on one end, and round flat rubber washers, such as compressed tennis balls or pieces of rubber tire, on the other end that are somewhat tight against the inside of the pvc pipe to act as "plungers" to suck the water up with when you pull back on the rod handle at the top of the pump.

My trusty home made clam pump – the only way to go!

The body of the pump (the three-inch pvc) has a hole on the side about one inch below the cap to allow air and trapped water to exhaust when you pull up on the pump handle. The cap itself has a small hole in the center of it on the top of the pump so the sucker rod can be inserted through it. On the top of the sucker rod will be a piece of three-quarter-inch metal pipe perpendicular to the rod as the pump handle. This will be about six inches long with holes midway through both sides of the pipe to allow the sucker rod to pass through to allow it to be attached. Thread a nut on the sucker rod threads along with a washer to where the threads end. Put the rod through the handle piece and thread another washer, lock washer, and nut on to squeeze the handle between them and the first nut and washer and tighten so that it is secure. A little Loctite would be helpful here, and then cut off the excess threaded rod for safety.

The rubber washers are attached much the same way on the other end of the sucker rod, but make sure that you attach them before you insert them and the rod in the pump body, as they will be up inside the pipe when the handle is attached after passing through the hole in the cap.

Lastly, you need a way to hold on to the pump body when you are pumping because holding the three-inch pipe in your hand can be somewhat awkward. An easy fix for this is to attach a piece of three-quarter-inch flat bar across the center of the cap so that it hangs out a couple of inches on each side of the pump. You will drill a hole in this just the same as you did the top of the cap because they will "line up" on top of each other and the sucker rod will pass through them both. This flat rod will be attached firmly to the cap before it is glued on with small nuts, washers, and bolts, which will require holes being drilled in the flat bar to fit these. This also has the added benefit of protecting the plastic cap from being worn out quickly from the bar passing back and forth during the pumping.

Another good fix for the handle issue is to drill a small hole in the body of the pump six to ten inches from the top of the cap and insert a five-inch bolt from the inside with a washer. Find or make either a metal or wooden handle so the bolt can go through the center of it and put a washer and nut on the outside of that handle to hold it in place.

Now, the fun part—how to properly use this magnificent device! First, find the clam! Wait until the tide is well on its way out but about forty-five minutes before ebb tide. This is because the clam pump uses water to blow its way down to the clam, not to suck the mud out, so you need to have a few inches of water over the mud flat where you are clamming. Walk along, and when you think you see the clam's mouth sticking up, which is usually just a small oddity in the sand or maybe the two "nostrils" showing, shove you finger in the hole. If it is a clam, you will feel a somewhat slimy creature immediately withdraw down into the hole away from your finger. Put the pump bottom over the hole and suck up the water, quickly blowing it out into the sand and mud. Do not push down on the pump; if anything, hold it up from the sand a little. Your pump will sink several inches. Repeat this until you feel the clam's hard shell with the pump body. You then reach down the hole and feel for the clam as well as all around, as many times two or three can be taken from one hole. Once you get the hang of it, you can hold the pump up and pump rapidly with one last big "suck" and spit the clam out in front of you. You may still have to feel for it or wait for the water to clear as you move to the next one because the water is too muddy from all the pumping to see it lying in front of you. Matter of fact, when you are all done pumping clams, take a walk through the area after a few minutes, and when the water clears you will almost certainly find a few more clams near the holes that you dug.

You will have your limit in just minutes while you watch the shovel brigades out there forever working their you-know-whats off! Be prepared to explain how you built that magic tool because these folks will surely be questioning you on one of their many rest breaks.

Now for the clam chowder, clam strips, and raw clams with lime and wasabi! Hold on!!! You have to clean them. This takes longer than the pumping but goes quick with a few jokes, beer, passing gas, or whatever your mode of cheap entertainment is.

To clean a clam, there are basically two parts. By that, I mean the body and the neck. First, you get the body out of the shell by sliding your sharp knife along the shell on the inside of both halves of the clam to cut the "scallop" muscle that attaches the clam to the shell. Then remove the neck from the body where the rough "skin" of the neck begins. Dip the neck in nearly boiling water for just a few seconds to scald it. Then, peel the brown skin from the neck and any remnants from the body to expose the snow-white meat. Cut the neck nearly in half for its full length and rinse it all well to avoid that "gritty" feel in your mouth when chewing. This is simple, but when you have fifty or a hundred clams in front of you and everyone scatters to beaches and outhouses to avoid the work, it takes some time! Now clam away, my friend!

More clam-digging tips

Learning how to dig for clams is pretty simple, but I will elaborate here a little for you. Digging for horseneck clams, Washington clams, softshell clams, and for geoduck clams is very similar and is the focus of the clam-digging articles in this book. Digging clams is fun for the whole family, and learning how just takes a little practice at finding clams to dig, having the clam pump, and learning the best way to dig them.

When learning how to dig clams, finding clams to dig is the first place to start. Find a bay that is a known clam-digging area. The folks at the local bait shop can usually tell you where the best clam-digging places in your area are. You can also check with your local fish and game department, who will certainly know where the best spots for clam digging near you are. While you are checking with them, you can find the clam-digging regulations and clam limits for the different types of clams as well. We all know that the game rules change as often as I change my underwear (maybe more often!), so don't rely on what someone tells you or what you learned from your last trip.

The best time to dig clams is when there is a very low tide, preferably a "minus" tide. You can find those on any good tide table booklet that they sell in the tackle shops or very easily online for free. You will want to get to the clam digging location prior to the tide reaching its lowest point so that the clam bed has a couple of inches of water over it to allow your clam pump to work properly.

Clam digging requires the proper clam-digging tools. Many folks use a shovel for digging clams, but the best way to dig clams by far is by using the clam pump–period! Using a shovel to dig clams is not a science. You find them and dig down to them. They do not "run" from you, they simply suck their neck down into their hole a foot or more. Usually the clams are thick enough in numbers that when you dig a hole with a shovel, you can widen the hole outward from the center for a distance and obtain your limit instead of digging one clam at a time. With a clam pump, you suck up water and blow the sand and mud out of the way until you get to each clam, but that process takes thirty seconds and very little energy—especially when compared to digging with a shovel. Using the pump is explained fully in the above section about building a clam pump, so I won't elaborate on it here.

Recognizing clams to dig when you are searching for them on a mud flat is the key to your clam digging success. It is easy to do once you learn how to spot clam "nostrils" in the mud and sand. I call them nostrils because I picture the clam neck as a big nose with two nostrils in the end of it for breathing. In fact, this is their vent that is used for feeding and many other functions. Sometimes you can actually see the two holes in a little mound or indention or other irregularity in the sand, but often, you just see the irregularity. The trick is to shove your finger in each suspect clam hole and see if you feel the slimy little bugger and feel him pull his neck down away from you. A lot of things make irregularities in the sand, and trust me, you don't want to dig and work your butt off for nothing, so make sure it is a clam.

When using a clam pump, finding clams to dig is done as the tide goes out in areas that still have a few inches of water over them so you can have water to suck up and blow out to make the clam pump work. You follow the water out as the tide goes out until it is all the way out. By that time, with a pump, everyone should have their limits! If you are digging clams with a shovel, you find clams for digging where it is high and dry, so to speak, because you don't want to have to dig in water! You will be beginning to clam dig when the clam diggers using clam pumps are heading back home.

Again, if you are going clam digging, make sure you read all the rules carefully. Most of the time each person has to carry their own clams in a separate bag or bucket than the others and often you are required to keep the first clams you get and not "trade up" for larger ones.

So now that you know how to dig clams, go clam digging and make some fried clam strips, clam sushi, and some clam chowder (both New England and Manhattan, of course).

Using a poke pole for eels and rockfish – I dated a girl in college with that same face!

Monkey Faced Eel

Using a poke pole for catching eels and other rockfish in the ocean is truly a fun fishing activity. Catching eels with a poke pole requires little tackle or expense, like some types of fishing. You can also catch rockfish with a poke pole when you are catching eels because they hang out in the same rocky areas. Many folks use a poke pole for catching Cabezon fish, which are a delicacy. Learning how to use a poke pole for eel fishing is a very simple task that pretty much consists of shoving the pole under rocks and moving from hole to hole at low tide. Read on and learn how to make a poke pole for catching eels and rockfish, the best bait for catching eels with a poke pole, and how to fish with a poke pole when you are at the ocean.

Making a poke pole for rockfish and eels takes very little time. All you need is to find a straight bamboo pole about ten to fifteen feet long that is pretty stout. At the small end of it, you will wrap wire around it with about a four-inch loop in it to tie your line to. Make sure this wire is firmly attached to the pole. Tie about six inches of thirty to sixty-pound fishing line to the wire with about a number six octopus hook at the other end. That is it! Now some folks will attach a piece of metal rod for two or three feet to the bamboo for strength and tape it on. There is also a collapsible poke pole fishing rod that is great if you want to spend the money. Some folks just use a nice long surf-casting pole, like what you might use for striped bass fishing or for catching surfperch off of a beach, with a little line hanging out, which works fine. It is just that with a longer pole, you can reach more holes in the rocks at low tide, and that is what poke poll fishing is all about.

When using a poke pole for fishing, it is best to go when the tide is very low. Look at a tide table and find a good "minus" tide if you can, but don't be afraid to try it on a regular low tide. At the very low tides, the rocks are exposed everywhere for hundreds of yards, which makes for the best poke pole fishing area. When using a poke pole for catching eels and rockfish, there is no need to fish deep or near where the open ocean meets the rocks, but getting where the fish know they aren't going to get trapped out of water is important. You do want to go where there is water pretty much under all the rocks and not dry ocean bottom with little holes. There might be fish there, too, but very limited amounts compared to where there is more water. Monkey-faced eels and rockfish have a sense for not getting caught high and dry.

The best bait for fishing with a poke pole for eels and rockfish is squid. It stays on the hook real well because it has a rubbery texture and about every fish or eel in the ocean likes it. If you happen to be abalone diving, abalone guts are great, too, because everything loves abalone, including good old Garry who is writing this book. You can also use mussels and small crab you catch as well as shrimp if you have those and can't get squid or abalone. I just find the best bait for fishing with a poke pole is one that stays on because it is much less work.

Fishing with a poke pole once you are out in the right spot, which is a very rocky area with water pockets everywhere, is easy. Just put the pole tip with the bait dangling off it into the water under rocks in holes. You can see or feel where the holes are and weasel the bait in as far as you can. Let it sit for ten or fifteen seconds and maybe move it around a little as you feel around in the hole. If you don't feel a bite, try another hole nearby and just keep moving along and probing.

You will feel the fish bite on the poke pole. Eels and rockfish are pretty aggressive biters. When they do bite, let them bite for a few seconds and then pull back on the pole. Some folks give it a yank to hook the eel or fish. If you miss the eel or fish, put the bait back in; they will more than likely bite again and again until you hook them. This is a great activity for the kids as long as they are kept away from the surf and they are old enough to navigate the slippery rocks and boulders. Just being out there among the tide pools is worth the trip!

When fishing with a poke pole, you should have a gunnysack or something that you can put the fish in and attach to your belt for carrying them. Having a buddy to carry that bag is nice. You have to remember that you are walking on the most slippery seaweed-covered rocks that you can imagine, and you need your hands to catch yourself when you slip around and fall. Notice I said "when" not "if"! For this reason, it is not a good idea to go poke pole fishing alone at any time. You could break a bone, get a gash, or knock yourself out, and having a buddy could save your life.

Poke pole fishing for eels can be dangerous in other ways as well. The ocean is rough, and about every ten thousandth wave is a rogue wave that is abnormally large. These can sweep you or your children into the ocean and out to sea before you know it. Keep in a well-protected area and a safe distance from where the waves are breaking into the rocks. A wave can sweep you off your feet and knock you out when your head hits a rock, and you could drown in six inches of water. Also, when you are poke pole fishing, you must make sure the tide doesn't come in and trap you out on the rocks. You might get there at low tide, walk out a hundred yards, and get to poke poll fishing, and time gets away from you. Then you go back and find that where you walked out to the rocks is now covered in several feet of water for fifty feet and rough. The hike down to the ocean can be quite a hike over steep terrain as well, and make sure you keep you and the kids away from the ledges up on top of the bluffs because the edges cave in often from the erosion from the wind and surf.

Rock picking abalone on a low tide

Rock picking abalone is a fun and rewarding sport when you are at the ocean in Northern California. You can get them without diving and while only wearing your jeans and tennis shoes! Getting abalone off the rocks when there is a minus tide allows people of all ages to enjoy getting abalone without diving for them. Abalone are huge water snails that attach themselves to the rocks under the water. When the tide is extremely low, which happens a few times a year, the abalone are actually out of the water in some places, and getting them while walking to them is called "rock picking." Don't get me wrong, they are not simply lying on the rocks. They are hidden in crevasses, between and underneath the rocks, and can usually only be found by feel and not by sight.

Rock picking abalone requires only a regulation abalone bar and a regulation measuring gauge, but having a wetsuit to wallow in the water comes in real handy because the water is cold and you will probably end up in it when you are rock picking abalone. Even though the tide is out and the rocky shore is exposed, it consists of thousands of little tide pools where the water is trapped in the rocks. It is extremely slippery and the rocks are sharp, so you have to be careful. Almost every inch is covered in some sort of seaweed or kelp, and you have to be careful of sea urchins, which are covered in sharp spines, much like a porcupine. A walking stick can be a handy tool, and moving slow is a must.

When rock picking abalone, you will move out towards the ocean as far as you safely can without being swept into the ocean by a wave. The abalone are not in areas that are routinely exposed on normal low tides. They live entirely under the water and will only tolerate very rare and short periods of time where they are not under water, such as when the extreme minus tides are present. The further you get out towards the ocean, the less often the abalone are exposed to air and the more you are apt to find. These tides occur a few times a year, and many are at night, when it is both unpractical and illegal to harvest abalone.

Once in the desired area for rock picking abalone, you will begin to kneel or lie down and reach under the rocks and begin to feel for their shells. You may feel them move as they tighten their shell to the rock to protect themselves, but more often than not, they are already in this defensive position from being exposed to the air. You will feel the rocks and feel around everything that feels anything like an abalone shell so that you find the edge of the shell with your fingers and can verify that it is an abalone. Sometimes you can just see them, but often this is not the case, and feeling for them is a must. Once you do find an abalone on the rocks, you have to try to ascertain whether it is of legal size or not, which is not as easy as it sounds. You have your regulation abalone gauge with you, which is a "C"-shaped device that is 7 inches inside and is made to verify that the abalone is at or above the required seven-inch sized shell. If the short legs of this "C"-shaped device touch both sides of the shell at any point, the abalone is of legal size. If you can get this bar into the abalone while on the rock and you can get a good measurement, that is great. If not, you may want to measure the abalone with your palm and fingers to get a good idea that it is legal before you try to remove it. Notice that I said "try" because many times you are unable to do so for one reason or the other. You need to do your best to make sure the abalone is legal for two good reasons. One is that it will surely suffer trauma to its body and may very well die whether you get it off the rock or not, and the other reason is that you may spend thirty minutes or more getting it off the rock; if it is too small, you have wasted a big part of the limited time you have before the tide comes back in and you have to leave.

When rock-picking abalone, the rocks are close together and often you are reaching as far as you can and even jamming your head between the rocks or half under the water to find an abalone to rock pick. When you do find one, you may only have a couple inches to work with, which gives you next to no "prying" room. These abalone are hanging on the rocks for dear life, and it is like they are super glued a lot of the time. The more you try to get them off, the harder they hold on! Their shells are clamped tightly to the rocks, and it may be difficult to find a place to slide the tip of your abalone bar between it and the rock to begin your prying. Finding this little gap is of the utmost importance when rock-picking abalone. Without this, you might as well move along! I will also mention that I have seen many folks finally pry off a nice nine-inch, thick, meaty, abalone and then find that it is too big to come out of the gap at the mouth of the crevasse it is in. This is a bummer! But it happens more often than you think, as does failing to be able to remove the abalone, because these abalone know that you, otters, seals, and everything else under the sun is after their tasty meat and they use every trick in the book to protect themselves.

Sticking your hand under the rocks with reckless abandon is a little unnerving to a lot of folks. After all, there are strange creatures lurking everywhere in the ocean. There are crabs, anemones, fish, eels, and any number of things that might pop out. I have even found a few good-sized octopuses in my day in the tide pools (which went into the deep fryer!). But about the only thing that you should be concerned with is the good ol' spinney sea urchin laying there ready for you to jam your hand into. The rest are harmless, and you get used to it pretty quickly if you are not a true sissy! If this really bothers you, stay home and tat doilies or go golfing and watch out for those scary bees!

Make sure that each person has his or her own measuring gauge and regulation pry bar, as this is the law. Also, each person must have their own bag to carry their abalone in and they may not be mixed with your friend's. You may not get other's abalone either. You must possess a valid fishing license and abalone report card with the tags that are required to be firmly attached to each abalone and filled out immediately upon taking one, along with filling out the report card. The abalone must be kept in the shell and properly tagged until being prepared for cooking. This means in the shell and tagged in your freezer at home until you thaw it to cook it. Trust me, this is the only way to freeze them anyway because they die with all their fluids in them and it keeps their flavor. Their meat may stain green or pink from the kelp in their gut when you do thaw them, but this hurts nothing. Right now, the limit is three per day and three in possession and no more than twenty-four in any one year. This means that if you have three at home in your freezer that are yours, you have your limit and may legally take no more until those are gone. The fines for breaking abalone laws are severe. Usually they confiscate all of your abalone gear (worth hundreds of dollars), give you a fine in the $2000.00 or more range, take your fishing license for three years, and give you three years' probation. Some offenses, such as selling them, can involve fines in the tens of thousands of dollar ranges and jail time and they may seize your car or truck. Repeat offenders may very well serve a little time in the slammer! It is a highly protected resource, and if you can't live within the law, you should find another hobby.

Rock picking abalone is a truly fun activity that even the kids can enjoy. I have been an avid abalone diver for over forty years, and I still love to rock pick. Diving, by far, is the typical way to get abalone, but rock picking is a popular sport as well. When diving, scuba tanks are not allowed. You must hold your breath and dive to get them by law. There is a very in-depth article on how to dive for abalone here in this book that is a good read for both the diver and the curious.

Remember, the ocean is powerful, unforgiving, and can be dangerous. Wave height changes with each wave, and freak waves happen all the time, so you have to be vigilant and alert at all times. Keep your eye on the ocean and have someone with you to do just that for the whole gang. The tide went out and it will come back in shortly. Always remember to get out before the tide comes up and the ocean blocks your escape route. Many times you came down a little ravine and the shore is all cliffs elsewhere. If the water blocks this escape or the surf comes up and makes it impassable, you are in trouble. A cell phone is handy for safety. Keep an eye on each other, especially children. Don't take very young kids, let them grow a while. Go light on the drinking of alcohol the night before and while you are rock picking abalone as well. Keep your eye out in the tide pools for rock crab when you are out there because they are excellent on the dinner table and there are a lot out there. This low tide is also a great time to "poke pole" for eels and fish, also, and you should check that section here in this book for sure. Knowing my ocean fishing tips can cause you to have the most fun you have ever had with your clothes on while you are at the ocean!

Catching rock crab in tide pools

Rock Crab – a tasty treat

Every sportsman should know how to catch rock crab if you visit the ocean. There are several ways to catch rock crab that do not involve a trap. Catching rock crab is a pretty entertaining activity, and you get some of the sweetest crab meat that you can find. This article explains how to catch them at low tide in the tide pools, which is fun for the whole family!

Rock crab are abundant in the ocean and bays. There are various species that are referred to as bay crab, red crab, as well as rock crab, but there is very little difference between them in looks or flavor. They live in the rocky areas of the ocean as well as throughout the shores and mud flats of the bays where they have some sea grass or seaweed for cover.

Catching rock crab in tide pools is something that you should learn just so you can take friends, and especially kids, to do when the tide is real low. A good minus tide is best. Just make sure you find a huge flat area with a lot of rocks and sand spots between them that is protected from the surf so there is zero danger of a wave washing anyone into the ocean and that you won't be trapped on if the tide comes in and your exit becomes blocked by water. You just walk around and look at the base of the rocks where they meet the sand, as the rock crab hunker down, half buried, in this area for protection when they find themselves trapped in a tide pool when the tide goes out. You might have to lift the seaweed up to see this area much of the time. You will see the back of the shells of the rock crab, and they look a lot like a rock, so you have to keep your eye peeled for them. Then you pull them up with your finger on the edge of the shell to see which end is the one without the pinchers, grab them by the other end, and toss them in your bucket. Grab them by the back two legs with one hand between your thumb and forefinger gently, but firmly enough to hold them without snapping their legs off. For some reason, they put their claws out in front of them and freeze in that position for a moment, but when they unfreeze, they come after you with their claws with gusto!

It is a kick, and you might find everything from sea urchins, abalone, to octopus in these tide pools to make dinner out of! This is one of my favorite ways to get rock crab. I like this method because it is fun watching kids, and even grown-ups, scour the ocean and get their own seafood to eat. A lot of times, we fill our buckets up with mussels for a good chowder feed when we are out catching rock crab, which is a great "two-fer"! Also, sometimes we take a fishing pole with us and cast out while we are catching crab because these rocks can be a great place to shore fish the ocean. Just being at the ocean and exploring the tide pools is rewarding and true fun, so getting the crabs is a huge bonus.

So, now you know how to catch rock crab and have fun at the ocean at low tide in the tide pools. You are ready to go!

Catching rock crab on mud flats at low tide

One time my nephew, my brother, and I were over at a small bay on the north coast of California, digging for Washington clams and horseneck clams, and we discovered a new way of catching rock crab along the edges of the exposed mud flats at low tide.

When you dig horsenecks, you have to get them when the tide goes out and usually on a minus tide. The mud flats that they live on are usually under two to six feet of water, except for when the tide is extremely low, such as on a "minus" tide. On one particular minus tide when we were there, we finished digging clams with our clam pumps and went to rinse off in the water on the edge of the mud flat we were on. I waded out to just over my waist and I bumped something hard with my foot. I thought it was probably a moon snail, which are good eating but not legal to take in our area. I reached down and I could feel a shell in the mud on the bottom. I then thought it might be some sort of seashell that might be neat, so I put my fingers under the lip of the shell to pry it out of the mud and I felt it raise one end on its own! I then felt the crab claws extend outward from that end as the crab assumed a defensive position. It kind of gave me a rush for a second!

I could feel which end the claws were on, and so I knew that the other end was the place to grab it. When I am abalone diving and spear fishing, I catch a lot of rock crab. When I catch them with my hands while diving, I have learned that when you grab their last two legs gently so they don't break off, that they kind of get a little paralyzed and just lock up with their claws straight out in front of them. Now, the second that you remove that rock crab from the water, this is no longer true, and you better have a bucket ready to put them into because they will be trying to get a hold of you with one of their big, strong claws. So, I slid my hand off the backside and found those two back legs and lifted the crab up out of the water. I got a better hold on him so I could check him out. It was a huge male rock crab, which is a keeper and an eater! You can tell the male rock crab from the females by looking at their tail on the underside of their shell. The females have wide tails (3/4 inch to an inch or so), and the males are much thinner. It may be illegal to keep the females in your area, but it is good practice in order to sustain the rock crab population to throw the females back regardless of the regulations. In this area, the rock crab must be four inches across the back of the shell from side to side to be legal.

After finding this rock crab, I started kind of walking around in the same depth of water and patting my feet on the bottom while I kind of half floated in my wetsuit that I wore to keep warm while clam digging. Next thing I knew, I found another. Then another. We were on to something!

We floated and patted are way along the edge of the sand bar and filled up two five-gallon buckets full of huge rock crab. Now, my nephew was remarkable at patting his feet and finding them, but when he did he would look up with a grin and say in a commanding voice "G'wan," meaning "go on," because he wasn't about to shove his hand into the murky water with some vicious monster of a five-inch little crab and get his little sensitive pinkie pinched! Sissy! Same with my brother. So here we were, the three of us side by side, half floating and patting our feet like we were doing some sort of Irish line dance. My nephew or brother would find one and the air would ring with what became to be a quite familiar sound of "G'wan"! We had our wetsuits on, and they are very buoyant, so my nephew offered to hold me down under the water so I could get the crab without having to struggle. His idea of how long it takes to get a crab was somewhat longer than the actual time it would take, and a couple of times I thought they were going to have to give me CPR, which I am sure they would have so they didn't have to risk life and limb catching a vicious, pit-bull-like five-inch terrifying beast!

That night we had a huge crab feed in the campground along with our clam chowder and fried clam strips. There isn't a lot of meat in the bodies of rock crab, but enough to eat for sure. However, their claws are huge and loaded with amazingly sweet crabmeat. You steam them like any other crab and serve them with melted butter, Italian salad dressing, cocktail sauce, or just plain! I have never seen anyone do this besides me and my family. Now you know how to do it, so "G'WAN"!

OTHER FUN AND OFF-THE-WALL FISHING

Frog gigging – a dying sport

Author holding a bull frog

NOT JUST FISHING

Frog gigging is a sport that requires a degree of devotion that most sportsmen just don't seem to have any longer. I think a lot of it is that the taste buds of the modern fisherman have evolved toward a reluctance to eat out-of-the ordinary foods that wasn't there when times were rough. It is amazing how many of my friends won't even try frog legs, while they are my very favorite food on this planet. Matter of fact, they are a favorite of my whole family, and when I was growing up, they were something that we would hide from each other so that we could have them all, just like the one chicken gizzard on the barbeque or the fried perch roe that never made it from the stove!

The devotion part I mentioned is because frog gigging is a sport that is done at night and into the early morning hours. Many an all-nighter has been pulled by my froggin' family in our quest for these tasty amphibians. And the darkest nights are best, as the moon illuminates you and the gig as you sneak up on them, so walking through the weeds and stinging nettles along the ditch banks becomes quite challenging. These nights can be made more pleasant if you opt to gig out of a boat in a slough or canal, although this can be dangerous because I have found that the professional frog gigger seems to require whisky breaks quite regularly.

First thing to know is that the frogs hibernate in the winter, so there is no use chasing them at that time of year. Second thing of importance is that they come out in the spring to breed and stock up their bellies for the next winter. When they are courting each other, they croak with full gusto. Matter of fact, during this time of year, the best way to find a place to gig frogs is to drive in an area near ditches, canals, sloughs, creeks, ponds, and such bodies of water and just shut off your car from time to time and listen. You can hear the music of the frog mating songs from very far off, and you head to them. Now, remember that these bullfrogs don't breed year round, and sometimes they just aren't in the mood, it seems, and they don't make much noise. You might hear just one lonely bullfrog but find the ditch he is in loaded with them. Or maybe you'll never hear a thing. In any case, if you are gigging canals and ditches by driving from one to the other, you should always check the ends of them where they flow under the road. Frogs seem to like these areas. Many times, we will take off right after dark and drive to a few of these ditch ends and gig two or three at several of them—enough for a quick snack and a little fun. If there are frogs at these ditch ends, it is very likely more of them can be taken in that ditch. Frogs are a funny beast. They have their likes and dislikes and idiosyncrasies. Usually, on a long ditch, they will be near one end or the other, and ninety percent of them will be on the same side of the ditch.

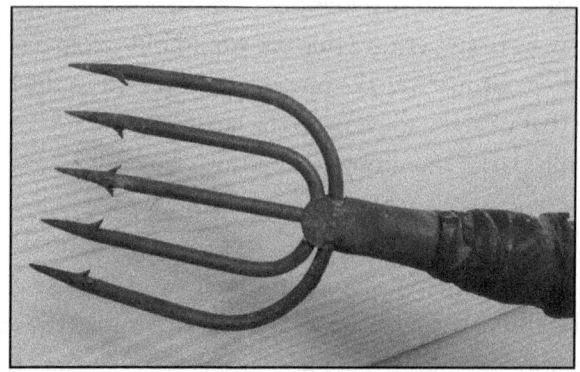

Frog gig

Before we get to the techniques, we need to discuss the gear you need. First, you need the frog gig. This is a four- or five-pronged, fork-like spear about the size of your open palm. They can be bought at most decent sporting goods shops but are often mislabeled as "fish-spears," which irks my butt. They have a round cavity on them so that you can insert the pole into it, which is never supplied with the gig, nor do they sell such a thing separately. This part of the device is made or acquired by the frog angler and often requires creativity in both obtaining it and attaching it to the gig. And the length is very important because the areas you plan to catch frogs in and whether you will be in a boat or not dictates your specific needs. In a boat, you need only a gig about ten feet long, but if you are gigging in a deep, steep-sided ditch, you may need twenty feet of pole, and there are plenty of in-between needs you might run into. Now, my nephew and I have at least three or four different gigs for all of our favorite places, and we use them all. Granted, that long twenty footer is hard to control, and you miss half of the frogs with it, but these are frogs that without it you would not have had even a chance to get anyway. And these ditches often hold the most frogs because they are so inaccessible. Some people will use good strong bamboo for the longer poles and maybe a long window-washing squeegee handle for the shorter ones. I have even seen metal electrical conduit used. It must fit in the round pocket on the gig, which has holes to screw it to the pole, which you should do first. Then, we like to take black electrical tape and wrap the holy you-know-what out of the gig and pole where they meet for a foot or so for added strength. Using that yellow shrink-wrap plastic stuff that is made into a tube that slips over the pole and is then shrunk with a blow dryer or torch around the whole pole is a huge plus for strength. The frogs aren't so hard on them, but falling and catching yourself with the pole is inevitable, and helping to guide the boat when the other person is running the trolling motor happens, too, due to excitement and whisky when you all of a sudden see a frog. This is known as "rudderin'," and I know this because my nephew screams for me to "quit rudderin'" over and over as the night progresses, and I have had my butt chewed for an hour while he repairs the gig from me so doing! You should use a file on the points of the gig to keep them sharp. When you gig a frog that is floating in the water, the gig will push him down instead of penetrating if it is not sharp, which you don't want. Missing a frog can cost you your position at gigging and cause immense ridicule!

Next, you must have a bright light. Notice that I said "you." If you go out with one light, somebody is without, and this situation causes extreme anxiety to that "nekkid" soul! You will find yourself saying "let me see that light for a second" a hundred times, which will be denied by the light-endowed angling partner you are with, trust me. If you do get the light from him, you will inevitably abuse your privilege and soon will be denied any further enjoyment of his light. Here, you will experience the feeling of "nekkedness"!

Make sure the light is bright and will stay that way, and that it has a focused beam to spot the shine of the frogs' eyes along with the white of their chins, and to blind them with so the person gigging can sneak the spearhead to within inches of them, which you must do. I like a big Mag-lite. Carry extra batteries, too, just in case.

Next, you need what we call an "HTFB"—a high-tech frog bucket. This would be one of those fish baskets with the spring-loaded tops. This replaces the gunnysack and holds those frogs in because they are impossible to kill.

Even when they have that huge spear right through their head and heart when you pull them from the water, they will still have one toe hung on the gig trying to push themselves off of the barbs that hold them on. You yank them off the gig and put them in the HTFB and they are still looking for an opening the next morning when you are reaching in the basket to get one to clean! They are ten times worse than when you spear fish. The fish only fight at first, the frogs plot and plan a jailbreak all night like the guys on *OZ*! (high tech frog bucket)

Frogs in the "HTFB"

Now, when you are walking the canal or in a boat in the backwaters of the delta, or wherever you are after frogs, you usually spot their eyes shining in the light like you see when you see a cat or a coon in the headlights from far off at night. If you are close, you usually see the yellow-white color of their skin under their mouths, but sometimes if they are facing away from you and floating in the water, you see a "bump" in the water that, upon closer inspection, is a bullfrog. At that point, one person holds the light very still right on the frog. The other person maneuvers the gig slowly to within six or less inches from the frog at a different angle than the light is hitting him from. Then, with a snapping and firm thrust, you "put the wood to him!" Especially if he is floating and you don't have the bank to push against to fully sink the gig to the hilt. Again, a dull spearhead is a huge problem in open water.

If you are on a ditch, it is best to have one person on each side so you can spot the frogs, as the ones on your side are against the bank in the weeds and you can't see them most of the time while your buddy across the ditch can. Here, we often just throw the gig back and forth over the ditch to who needs it next. Another hint is to stop and listen when you can't find the frog you hear. Sooner or later he will croak, and you can pinpoint him in the weeds. They often will sit in the weeds and grass in the water and let you move in aside with the gig, even moving them a little, to allow you to find them. It is odd but they do.

In closing, I want to address the scads of people out there that will inevitably tell their story of how they used to use a red cloth on a treble hook and dangled it in front of the frog, and the frog would bite it and they would get frogs that way. I have done this a thousand times; it is fun and can be done in the daytime. It doesn't need to be a red cloth; anything that moves will work. I like hula poppers, jitterbugs, bombers, or any lure. Those damn frogs will swim right after them for several feet to get them. They will eat anything. We have taken everything from several huge crawfish to baby muskrats out of their stomachs when we were cleaning them. Anyway, this lure fishing for frogs is fun but tedious, and good for the amateur who doesn't eat a bunch of legs like we do, as the amount of frogs you catch is a fraction of what a good gigging night will yield. Our one night record is 108 huge frogs. In case you are bad at math, that would equate to 216 enormous frog legs!

Oh, and another hint I wanted to tell you has to do with cleaning. When you clean them, most people just eat the rear legs. My cousin and most oriental folks slice them around the neck and eat the front legs, loins, and the rear legs. Regardless, when you go to clean them, they will be alive. Grab them in one hand firmly by the legs, swing them, and whack their head hard on a rock, tree, or something. Their legs and body will stiffen as if rigor mortis has set in within one second. This makes the slicing of the skin hugely easier and seems to calm the crap out of the frog, too! Try it if you think I am B.S.ing you.

To cook them, make sure you use a deep fryer. It is so much better than just frying them because they just soak up grease and don't get crispy on the outside. Don't use batter, either—on frogs or any fish you fry. Just wet them with water and bread them by rolling them in a mixture of seasoned breadcrumbs, cornmeal, and flour with some garlic powder (not garlic salt – throw it away if you own it), and salt and pepper to taste. Also, it is best to soak the frog legs in salt water for five to ten minutes before cooking and then rinse them to minimize them "jumping" in the pan. The salt water tweaks the nerves and takes it out of them. Like any game, it is best to eat them later in the day after you clean them to let the cleaning aromas dissipate from your nasal and oral palate's memories to make your dining experience all it can be.

I didn't write about gigging from a boat much, as it is pretty self-explanatory. Just use a nice flat-bottomed boat that you and your partner can lift in and out of ditches and such. Oars are okay, but a trolling motor is nice. Don't forget the ice chest!

Jugging for snapping turtles and catfish

Tasty snapping turtle

When I was back in Ohio, I went "jugging" for snapping turtles and big catfish in the backwaters of the Ohio River that were created from the rise in the water level when they put the locks and dams in the river so big barges could navigate it. The little creeks that ran from the surrounding hills in West Virginia and Ohio into the river became what we call sloughs out here in the delta of Northern California. They became still and protected backwater habitat for the turtles and catfish to thrive in.

Unlike out here, you are allowed to leave your fishing poles un-attended; this "jugging," as it were, is a great and effective way to fish. There isn't much to it, either.

You get a few Clorox type jugs for floats and tie a leader, preferably steel line or even bailing wire, to the handle; it should be three or four feet long with a good-sized hook or treble hook on the bottom of it. Bait it up with chicken liver, or some other bait of your liking, and toss it out in this still backwater to float freely overnight. Do this a few more times and head to the next creek in your boat. Do the same and move along. You have to put your name and fishing license on each jug. This may not even be legal any longer because it has been many years since I was back there, so you will need to check the fish and game regulations on this type of fishing.

You come back and find the jugs and lift them to see if you have that huge catfish or snapping turtle or some other tasty fish on your line. Sometimes, you don't even have to look because the jug is moving around with the fish or half sunk by a turtle pulling down on it, or it is a long way from where you left it. You pull it in carefully because that turtle is going to be pissed, and he has a big mouth that is going to want a piece of you! My brother's friend had an arm missing and had a hook on it. Surprisingly enough, his nickname was—you guessed it—Hook. Hook would hold his hook out and let the turtle bite it with his mouth while my brother held the turtle's body. Hook would stretch the turtle's head out over the boat seat or a piece of wood, and either my brother or Hook would hack it off so the risk of getting bit was gone and you could ride in the boat without risk to "Big Jim and the twins"!

This is some great backwoods, fun, exciting, good old boy, hillbilly fishing! Then the eating gets going on the riverbank with your poles casted in the main river and the campfire blazing for some good times! These turtles have seven distinctly different types of meat in them and make for some great vittles, and fishing for them makes for some fun times! Try it out!

Catching crawfish out of rice fields by hand and with traps in rivers

Author catching crawfish in rice field

Nothing is more fun than dumping a huge pot of fresh steamed crawfish in the middle of the table and pinchin' tails and suckin' heads with all your friends. Everyone starts calling in the late summer and starts asking if it's Crawdad Season yet. There is no defined "season" in the law, and the friends are really asking if they have started draining the rice fields yet because that is the time when thousands and thousands of pounds of these delicious little mini-lobsters gather at the rice gates between the fields for the taking. I have been asked so many times about how we get these crawdads like this that I wanted to include a lesson on that in this book for those of you who live in or are visiting an area where rice is grown.

The rice grows in water several inches deep all summer long. The water can't be too shallow or too deep or the seeds won't form in the pods. Great care is taken to make those fields flat as a pancake. Levees are built with the contour of the land so the drops in elevation only take place through a wooden box or a culvert pipe called a gate. Each divided portion of the field is called a check. When the water drops through, it usually digs out a small area just below the gate that holds water for a week or two after the rest of the field is dried up. All the crawdads find this water, and sometimes there might be two hundred pounds of them in one little pool the size of a twin bed and a foot deep. The whole thing is red with crawfish! Many times, there are just fifty or a hundred, but when you find them at one gate in the field, the others are probably loaded, too, so it doesn't take long to get a meal. So you know, each field usually gets water from a ditch (sometimes a pump), and that water runs from check to check, and I can tell you that the hole where the water dumps from the ditch into the field is usually the best place by far. They are easy to hunt down because you can drive on the levee next to the ditch and just look down at each fill pipe. In the checks, you have to get out and walk to each one and check it for 'dads.

Many fields, and some checks in fields, have not one crawdad in them. Often, the biggest hassle is driving around an hour until you find a "honey hole," and then you are done in thirty minutes with two ice chests full and knowledge of a place to get more for several days until the water dries up or turns stagnant. When you are driving around, many of the gates have crawdads, but the water is too high and the crawfish can swim away too fast. Go elsewhere but make a mental note that this field is "getting ripe"! It is part of the game. When the season is on, we eat these rice crickets several times a week because in a month or a little more, it's all over till the next year.

Typical afternoon catch of crawfish

Now, how do you get them once you have found them? First, you can't be a crybaby sissy! You just wade in the pool with some old tennis shoes you got at the Goodwill (I go barefoot) and start grabbing them and throwing them one by one in your bucket, making sure each one is alive. When your bucket is full, you dump it in a huge ice chest and back you go. When you grab them, there is an area on their back, right behind their eyes, that you can grab, and they can't pinch you. This area, oddly enough, is rough and above the tail and looks as though it was designed to be used to grab them. You can also grab them by both pinchers tightly and they can't get you. But do not be a sissy—you will get pinched and it hurts a little, sometimes a little more than a little! But it is bearable. My friends and I grab them by the handfuls and stick our hands in holes and yank them out, and there is a lot of cussin' going on. But late in the year when the gates are all pretty dry and you are hungry for crawdads, you have to do some noodling in their holes or do without! Some people use BBQ tongs to get them, and I would suggest a pretty pink dress to go with them!

You can get crawfish year round in the lakes and rivers if you use traps. These are the "blues," which are usually larger and come out of clear water. Unlike the reds and greens that are found in the rice fields, these do not burrow or hibernate. These crawfish live in the rocks; areas where a levee has been "riprapped" with rocks for its protection are a great place for your traps. When I go striper fishing or sturgeon fishing, I like to set some traps in the area and go for a "two-fer"! If I am going fishing the following day, I will leave the traps out overnight because the crawfish are nocturnal for the most part.

Crawfish trap

Another way I get these blue crawfish is by using my diving mask and snorkel in the mountain streams when I am up there trout fishing. I throw a can of dog food with holes poked in it upstream from a slower-moving area, and the crawfish come out of their hiding places in the rocks looking for the food. Sometimes the bottom comes alive with them, and I will catch hundreds with my hands! It's a great way to cool off in the summer and some cheap entertainment!

When you get these little tasty mudbugs home, rinse them with the hose and dump the ice chest out, holding the lid down, and then let the hose run full speed on them for a half hour or so with something sitting on the lid to hold it down so the water can flow out and the crawdads can't. If you save some for the next day, do this all again and sort out the dead ones. Don't leave them soaking in still water or they all will die. Storing them in gunnysacks under a lawn sprinkler is ideal for storing them a couple days.

Cooking them is easy. Just get a huge pot with a lid and boil the water on an outdoor cooker if you plan to stay married. When it is boiling, reach into the ice chest with both hands and grab as many as you can hold and toss them in until the pot is full. Keep the kids away because the water is hot and there is a lot of cussing at this point, too, from grabbing into a full ice chest of pinchers with reckless abandon. Just bring the water back to a boil and cook them about fifteen minutes until they are bright red. Hold the lid on the pot with a crack and strain the water out, but be careful because the steam will fry your hands and face very quickly. And watch your feet, too. Some people throw in some Zatarans Crab Boil or some Old Bay Seasoning and some corn on the cob, which is good. But the trick is the dips that you use. Chop up scads of garlic and cook it without burning it in real butter and dip the crawfish like lobster. They taste better than lobster. We also have a cocktail sauce on the table made with ketchup, horseradish, Worcestershire sauce, and a little garlic that is outstanding. The wine choice with this meal is usually whisky and beer!

We always spread scads of newspaper in layers on our granite counter and dump them out on it, and everyone stands or sits around and yanks the tails and pinchers off to eat and throws the bodies and shells in a pile in the center. When the meal is over, we just fold it all into the newspaper and slide it into the trash can and out it goes. We do the same for crab. A one-step clean up!

A little trick to show off your eating skills is to pinch the tail off and use your thumb and index finger on one hand to straighten the tail out while firmly pinching and rolling the other thumb from the tail's end up, forcing the tail meat out in one motion in one second. This takes practice but it is worth it to irritate your friends that are sitting there picking shells for thirty seconds to get one little morsel. Also, sometimes you can pop the movable claw out and the meat comes with it, or you can suck the meat right out of the claw after dipping it in butter. The claws taste like crab and are worth the work. This is some real fun for the whole family!

SOME OTHER EXCELLENT FISHING TIPS FOR YOU

Using a trailer hook when trolling – great for bass and trout

Using a trailer hook when trolling with night crawlers, minnows, and other baitfish is a fishing technique that will prove extremely valuable in most cases. I do not attach the trailer hook to the minnow or night crawler. I let it freely dangle just at or behind the end of the bait I am using, and the movement through the water while trolling takes it back and even makes it have a little action to attract the fish. My dad always insisted that using a trailer hook that is hooked through the tail of the minnow or worm killed the action of both the bait and the trailer hook. He was one of the best fishermen that has ever crapped behind two shoes, or at least that's what he told me, and he caught a lot of fish trolling, so I have to just go with it! Some days we would go trolling with minnows in Lake Oroville in Northern California and come back with limits of German browns, rainbows, and salmon between two and eight pounds. Of those, we would catch eighty percent of them on the trailer hook and not the front hook, so who can argue!

The biggest reason for using a trailer hook when trolling is to catch the fish that bite the minnow or night crawler hard but too far back to get the front hook, which is in the mouth of the minnow or halfway down the night crawler. I wish I had a nickel for every time we lost our minnow on a good bite or missed a good bite and pulled the minnow in to see where the scales were missing on the body where the fish hit it! That is how we figured out using a trailer hook when trolling in the first place.

Tying a trailer hook correctly (aka, my dad's way) is real simple. We would always use a treble hook much smaller than the front hook. We would just tie the front hook on the line normally and leave a tail of the line that it was tied to hanging out so the treble trailer hook could be attached at an area so it was at or further out than the length of our typical bait. That was it, and again it just dangled freely. Using a trailer hook for trolling for trout in a lake or trolling for any fish with baitfish is a great way to increase your success immensely!

A buddy of mine used to cast live crawfish for black bass when we grew up, and he would use the same setup except he would attach a trailer hook to the tail of the crawdad using a single, larger hook and come up through the top of the tail so the hook was facing towards the crawfish's head over its back. We were young, and lures were not in the budget! Matter of fact, we were so poor that my mom used to cut the pockets out of my and my brother's pants just so we would have something to play with!

How to bait minnows and baitfish for different purposes

Baiting minnows on the hook depends on the way you are fishing. A big factor in how to put minnows on a hook is whether the minnow will be sitting in one spot or whether you will be trolling with a minnow or using a minnow as live bait with a bait-casting rig.

Using minnows to fish for crappie is usually done by baiting the minnow through the body just below the back dorsal fin. When you put a minnow on the hook this way, make sure you just go deep enough to get a firm bite of the body without damaging the organs of the fish or breaking its back or tearing its flesh more than necessary. Use a sharp hook when baiting minnows for this reason, and so the hook sets in the fish's mouth easily. I know you're cheap, but avoid using those rusty old hooks that you find on the bottom of your tackle box for any kind of fishing! Matter of fact, you should always keep a fishhook sharpening stone in your tackle box.

If you are using a minnow to catch trout while trolling, baiting minnows is done through the mouth. When baiting minnows through the mouth, just like baiting any baitfish in the mouth, open the minnow's mouth and put the hook through the roof of the minnow's mouth near the lips so not too much damage is done to its head. Even though the trolling motion will make the minnow "swim," I like to fish with live minnows if at all possible. If you just put the hook in a minnow through both lips, you sew the mouth shut so it can't breathe, and it dies quickly. Baiting a minnow through the back as mentioned above drags it sideways through the water, and you are more apt to scare the fish than catch one!

When using a bait-casting setup and fishing with live bait for striped bass, baiting a minnow is a matter of preference between the two methods above. And when fishing with minnows for striped bass and other fish using live bait, I mean "live"! Do what you can to damage the minnow as little as possible with the hook. If you are using other baitfish that are large, it is best to thread the minnow with a hook threader up to the head from the tail and put the hook facing upwards above the head. The hook threader pushes the line just under the skin up to the head and out the skin where the hook is then tied on and the eye carefully reinserted back into the skin in the hole that the line came from.

Sometimes, we cast for striped bass in shallow moving water where it is flowing out of a pipe or floodgate or over a weir. Baiting minnows through the upper lip is the minnow baiting method I use for this type of fishing, but I have friends that bait them through the back.

Learning how to fish from scratch – some helpful guidance for the beginner

Author and family trout fishing and making memories

Learning how to fish is not difficult at all. The best way to learn how to fish is to keep it simple. You don't have to learn how to fish from a professional because learning how to fish can often best be done at the local "mom and pop" bait shop in your area. These folks that own the bait shop, along with the usual gang found there drinking coffee and shooting the breeze, usually know the best ways to catch fish in your particular area as well as what is biting at that particular time. For those just learning how to fish, these folks, in almost every case, will bend over backwards to help you learn about fishing. After all, you then become another customer for them and another person to tell their same favorite stories to that everyone else has heard dozens of times!

Learning how to fish from the folks in the local bait shop is one great way to learn how to fish, but there are other ways to learn about fishing from scratch. Every article here in this book is made for fishermen and women of all skill levels to learn how to catch particular fish in a way that is easy to grasp. You can learn to catch sturgeon, learn how to catch striped bass, along with about any other type of game fish. The sections on how to fish for bluegill and the one about catching mud catfish are great for the beginning fisherman, and especially kids, as they are found about anywhere and are easy to catch. There are even articles on getting sea urchins, crab, abalone, how to gig frogs, and about every type of fishing you can imagine in this book. The author has been fishing for fifty-five years, and he shares this experience with you in an easy-to-read, fun, and down-to-earth way.

Another good way to learn how to fish is to pick up some fishing magazines or visit your local library. If you have a particular type of fishing in mind, you can probably find a magazine that has articles about fishing for that type of fish. Here again, when learning how to fish, always start at the local bait shop so you can learn what types of fish are in your area and when the best time to fish for them is so you don't waste your time learning about fishing some fish that is only found ten states away! Also, when you begin learning how to fish, you may find a particular kind of fishing that sounds particularly fun to you, and you always want to learn how to fish for fish that are in your budget to fish for. After all, why learn how to fish from a boat when you don't have one and can't afford one? Fishing is not a cheap sport, but some types of fishing require only very inexpensive tackle and equipment. It is also nice to find fish that are found close to your home so you can enjoy fishing without driving far away.

Learning how to fly-fish is one type of fishing that I would suggest a lesson from someone who has some experience. Fly-fishing involves numerous types of fishing line and tackle depending on the type of fishing, time of year, location, and scads of other variables. Learning to fly-fish also involves learning how to cast a fly rod, which is an art. Any local fly-fishing club will probably have a member that would be glad to help you learn how to fly fish, and many fly-fishing shops have regular free classes for the beginning fisherman. Here again, if that is something that interests you, ask who might help you learn how to fly fish at the local tackle shop.

Teaching kids how to fish is also something that you should do. It is a rare occasion that a kid doesn't like to fish, especially if you start them young. Fishing is an activity that may occupy your child or grandchild throughout their life and keep them on the right track through their teens. Teaching kids how to fish is something that can do nothing but good for their entire life—and for your relationship with them. Every kid wants to learn how to fish if just given the opportunity. I started fishing when I was four years old, and I love it today as much as ever.

Fish spawning temperature chart – a great chart for your shop wall

The key to catching fish when spawning is knowing the right places to look and the water temperature that triggers the fish to spawn. The fish will move into shallow water and search for a place to build their nests when that spawning temperature reaches the desirable point and they feed aggressively in the couple weeks prior to when they spawn, so knowing the right temperature when fish spawn is a great tool to have in one's tackle box of tricks. I have included a list of spawning temperatures for fish that are fished for sport most often, which I have gleaned from various information sources.

Most of the time the males are the nest builders as well as the ones responsible for guarding the nest and young fry from predators. You might find a female lingering near the nest from time to time, but she will not be inclined to bite a lure out of anger like the male will. You might tease her all day by dropping your lure on her nose and she will ignore it, while the male will try and kill it! In the spring, usually in April, the bass will spawn in very shallow water from about eighteen inches to three feet and are visible on their nests. "Sight fishing largemouth bass" and other fish is a popular technique for catching huge black bass by anglers, so you should check that article out here in this book. The bass might spawn several times in the spring, many times using the same nest, and a single male may have two or more nests from different females in the same vicinity at the same time, diligently guarding each. This is true of many fish.

Here is a list of some of the spawning water temperatures for the most popular game fish. The temperatures are in Fahrenheit.

Largemouth Bass	68-72
Smallmouth Bass	59-60
Spotted Bass	63-68
Yellow Bass	62-66
Cherokee Bass	55-57
White Bass	57-68
Striped Bass	59-65
Sturgeon	58-59
Muskie	49-59
Walleye	45-51
Northern Pike	40-52
Sauger	40-45
Paddlefish	50-55
Warmouth	75-80
White Crappie	60-65
Black Crappie	62-68
Bluegill	70-75
Green Sunfish	75-85
Red Ear	68-75
Channel Catfish	75-80
Blue Catfish	70-75
Flatheads	66-75
Bullhead Catfish	79-89
Carp	63-75
Rainbow Trout	50-55
Brown Trout	47-52
Brook Trout	45-48

These are typical temperature ranges where fish spawn, and almost every species will spawn several times during the spring and move from areas that are too warm into waters that are just right because too warm or cold of water is lethal to the various fishes' roe. The time of year that these fish spawn will vary by location due to the air temperature and other factors, so one state in the south, such as Texas, may see their fish spawning long before Minnesota, and you will see those up in some shallow pond spawn long before those in a moving river carrying the spring snowmelt. Using a thermometer to gauge water temperature at various depths might prove to be more handy than you realize. Anyway, good luck fishing, and a little catch and release of some of these fish when they are spawning is highly recommended.

www.ingramcontent.com/pod-product-compliance
Lightning Source LLC
Chambersburg PA
CBHW070809100426
42742CB00012B/2310